STRATEGIC STUDIES INSTITUTE

I0429396

The Strategic Studies Institute (SSI) is part of the U.S. Army War College and is the strategic-level study agent for issues related to national security and military strategy with emphasis on geostrategic analysis.

The mission of SSI is to use independent analysis to conduct strategic studies that develop policy recommendations on:

- Strategy, planning, and policy for joint and combined employment of military forces;

- Regional strategic appraisals;

- The nature of land warfare;

- Matters affecting the Army's future;

- The concepts, philosophy, and theory of strategy; and

- Other issues of importance to the leadership of the Army.

Studies produced by civilian and military analysts concern topics having strategic implications for the Army, the Department of Defense, and the larger national security community.

In addition to its studies, SSI publishes special reports on topics of special or immediate interest. These include edited proceedings of conferences and topically-oriented roundtables, expanded trip reports, and quick-reaction responses to senior Army leaders.

The Institute provides a valuable analytical capability within the Army to address strategic and other issues in support of Army participation in national security policy formulation.

THE SAUDI-IRANIAN RIVALRY
AND THE FUTURE OF MIDDLE EAST SECURITY

W. Andrew Terrill

December 2011

FOREWORD

The Middle East is undergoing an era of revolutionary change that is challenging the foreign policies of the United States and virtually all regional states. In this new environment, opportunities and challenges exist for a number of regional and extra-regional states to advance their national interests, while attempting to marginalize those of their rivals. Despite these changes, the Arab Spring and revolutions in countries such as Tunisia, Egypt, and Libya have not altered some of the more fundamental aspects of the Middle East regional situation. One of the most important rivalries defining the strategic landscape of the Middle East is between Iran and Saudi Arabia. The competition between these two states is long-standing, but it is especially important now. Political relationships that have endured for decades, such as the one between Iran and Syria, now seem to be in some danger, depending upon how current struggles play out. The stakes in this rivalry can thus become higher in an environment of revolutionary upheaval.

In this monograph, Dr. W. Andrew Terrill considers an old rivalry as it transitions into a new environment. Saudi Arabia and Iran have been rivals since at least the 1979 Iranian Islamic Revolution. As Dr. Terrill points out, this competition has taken a variety of forms and was especially intense in the aftermath of the Iranian revolution. Under Iranian President Mohammad Khatami (1997-2005), the rivalry relaxed to some extent, but a permanent détente was not possible because of a backlash within the Iranian political system. The successor presidency of Mahmoud Ahmadinejad further damaged relations and the Saudi-Iranian relationship was dealt an especially serious setback over the Saudi-led intervention into Bahrain. Because the current Saudi-Iranian rivalry is taking place in a variety of countries of interest to the United States, an awareness of the motivations and issues associated with the rivalry is important to U.S. policymakers. Dr. Terrill clearly identifies the struggle as region-wide, encompassing countries as far apart as Egypt, Bahrain, Yemen, Lebanon, Syria, and especially Iraq, where the United States is preparing to withdraw almost all of its troops. He also notes that while U.S. interests often overlap with those of Saudi Arabia, such is not always the case. Saudi Arabia and the United States often work well together in seeking to contain Iranian influence, but Saudi Arabia also is an absolute monarchy opposed to Arab democracy or any democratic reform of the existing monarchical systems.

The Strategic Studies Institute is pleased to offer this monograph as a contribution to the national security debate on this important subject, as our nation continues to grapple with a variety of problems associated with the future of the Middle East and the ongoing challenge of advancing U.S. interests in a time of Middle East turbulence. This analysis should be especially useful to U.S. strategic leaders and intelligence professionals as they seek to address the complicated interplay of factors related to regional security issues, the withdrawal of U.S. forces from Iraq, fighting terrorism, and providing for the support of local allies. This work may also benefit those seeking better understanding of long-range issues of Middle Eastern and global security. We hope this work will be of benefit to officers of all services, as well as other U.S. government officials involved in military and security assistance planning.

DOUGLAS C. LOVELACE, JR.
Director
Strategic Studies Institute

ABOUT THE AUTHOR

W. ANDREW TERRILL joined the Strategic Studies Institute (SSI) in October 2001, and is SSI's Middle East specialist. Prior to his appointment, he served as a Middle East nonproliferation analyst for the International Assessments Division of the Lawrence Livermore National Laboratory (LLNL). In 1998-99, Dr. Terrill also served as a Visiting Professor at the U.S. Air War College on assignment from LLNL. He is a former faculty member at Old Dominion University in Norfolk, Virginia and has taught adjunct at a variety of other colleges and universities. He is a retired U.S. Army Reserve Lieutenant Colonel and Foreign Area Officer (Middle East). Dr. Terrill has published in numerous academic journals on topics including nuclear proliferation, the Iran-Iraq War, Operation DESERT STORM, Middle Eastern chemical weapons and ballistic missile proliferation, terrorism, and commando operations. He is also the author of *Global Security Watch-Jordan* (Praeger, 2010). Since 1994, at U.S. State Department invitation, Dr. Terrill has participated in the Middle Eastern Track 2 talks, which are part of the Middle East Peace Process. He has also served as a member of the military and security working group of the Baker/Hamilton Iraq Study Group throughout its existence in 2006. Dr. Terrill holds a B.A. from California State Polytechnic University and an M.A. from the University of California, Riverside, both in political science, and a Ph.D. in international relations from Claremont Graduate University, Claremont, California.

SUMMARY

Saudi Arabia and Iran have often behaved as serious rivals for influence in the Middle East, especially the Gulf area, since at least Iran's 1979 Islamic Revolution and the 1980-88 Iran-Iraq War. While both nations define themselves as Islamic, the differences between their foreign policies could hardly be more dramatic. In most respects, Saudi Arabia is a regional status quo power, while Iran often seeks revolutionary change throughout the Gulf area and the wider Middle East with varying degrees of intensity. Saudi Arabia also has strong ties with Western nations, while Iran views the United States as its most dangerous enemy. Perhaps the most important difference between the two nations is that Saudi Arabia is a conservative Sunni Muslim Arab state, while Iran is a Shi'ite state with senior politicians who often view their country as the defender and natural leader of Shi'ites throughout the region. The rivalry between Riyadh and Tehran has been reflected in the politics of a number of regional states where these two powers exercise influence.

The 2011 wave of pro-democracy and anti-regime protests, now known as the Arab Spring, introduced new concerns for both Saudi Arabia and Iran to consider within the framework of their regional priorities. Neither government's vital interests were involved in the outcome of the struggle in Tunisia where the Arab Spring began, but both leaderships became especially interested in these events once the unrest spread to Egypt. While Saudi Arabia watched the ouster of Egypt's President Hosni Mubarak with horror, the Iranian leadership saw some potential opportunities. Riyadh's decision in late May to grant Egypt $4 billion in loans and grants quickly became a powerful incentive for Cairo to consider Saudi priorities, especially in light of Egypt's declining tourism revenues and the interruption of Western private investment in the Egyptian economy. Both nations are continuing their efforts to improve relations with post-Mubarak Egypt, although Saudi Arabia's financial resources give it an advantage in the struggle for influence.

Iran seeks to expand its power in the Gulf, which is a key area of competition between the two states. Saudi Arabia and to varying extents other Gulf Arab states often seek to contain Iran's quest for dominance. In the struggle for Gulf influence, Saudi Arabia has consistently maintained a vastly higher level of political clout with local states than Iran. Iran currently cannot hope to overshadow Saudi regional influence in the Gulf, but it does seek to influence Gulf Arab states and is especially interested in pressuring them to minimize or eliminate their military links to the West. In recent years, Sunni-Shi'ite tension in the Gulf seems to have been rising for a number of reasons. Such problems reached a high point with the March 2011 Saudi-led military intervention in Bahrain. Consequently, it is increasingly likely that the rivalry between Riyadh and Tehran will intensify in the near future. In this environment, U.S. intelligence officials and policymakers will correspondingly need to be aware of the possibility that Saudi Arabia may overestimate Iranian involvement in any regional crisis and at times conflate Shi'ite assertiveness with Iranian activism on the basis of their own form of worst-case analysis and very little evidence.

Iran's closest Arab ally has been Syria, and Tehran has been watching the 2011 popular unrest in Syria with considerable alarm. Syrian leaders sometimes believe that their country is or could become the junior partner in the relationship with Iran, and Damascus has disagreed with Tehran on a variety of important issues within an overall context of cooperation and friendly ties. The Syrian relationship with Riyadh is different. As a monarchy, Saudi Arabia has maintained a long tradition of distrust towards Syria, which defines itself as a republican and sometimes a revolutionary regime. While the Saudis have been willing to work with Damascus on occasion, they do not have much in common with the Syrian government beyond Arabism. More recently, both Saudi Arabia and Iran have needed to consider how Syrian unrest impacts upon their interests. Tehran clearly has the most to lose, and it is mostly standing by its Syrian ally. The previous Saudi détente with Damascus was significant, but Riyadh never viewed the Assad regime as an ally and could be expected to take some pleasure in seeing Tehran lose its most important Arab partner should this regime fall. On the negative side, Riyadh almost certainly would not view the turmoil in Syria as an unqualified Saudi victory even if the Assad regime was overthrown and replaced by an anti-Iranian government. The Saudi leadership remains ultra-conservative and, correspondingly, takes a dim view of both revolutionary upheaval and Arab democracy, although Riyadh would almost certainly seek to maintain a high level of influence with any post-Ba'athist government. If Syrian President Assad is overthrown, the United States may seek to work with Saudi Arabia and other friendly states to make certain that Syrian financial and military ties to Iran do not survive the transition.

In a major bid to enhance its regional influence, Tehran has attempted to portray itself as the leading power supporting Palestinian rights and opposing Israel through a variety of means, including supplying weapons and funding to Palestinian militants. Saudi Arabia has made numerous efforts to help the Palestinians and to use its financial resources and political influence on their behalf, but it has also served as the chief sponsor of an Arab League peace plan that is of interest to some Israeli leaders. Riyadh maintains normal political relations with both of the major Palestinian political parties, Fatah and Hamas, the latter of which has been designated a terrorist organization by the United States. Saudi influence with Hamas has declined steadily in recent years and been almost totally displaced by that of Iran. Elsewhere in the Levant, large numbers of Lebanon's Shi'ites consider Iran to be an important ally that has extended considerable support to the Lebanese in resisting what they define as Israeli aggression. In this environment, the United States will almost certainly wish to continue to pursue the Middle East Peace Process for both its intrinsic value and in order to undermine Iran's efforts to enhance its role in Lebanon and the Palestinian territories.

The future of Iraq is a central concern for both Iran and Saudi Arabia, as well as the United States. The planned withdrawal of U.S. troops from Iraq will also complicate the Saudi-Iranian rivalry in the region. The departure of U.S. troops may radically change the ways in which regional states help their Iraqi supporters. After the United States withdraws the remainder of its military forces from Iraq, it will be difficult for Saudi Arabia and the other Sunni Gulf monarchies to remain passive should Iran continue to arm Iraqi Shi'ite militias. One of the most troubling ways in which Iran exerts its influence in Iraq is through various Shi'ite militia organizations that engage in terrorism and strikes against U.S. troops and other targets inside Iraq. These pro-Iranian militias are sometimes called Special Groups. Iran has considerable influence with them and provides weapons and training to some of these forces through the elite Iranian Revolutionary Guards Corps' al-Quds Force.

Finally, U.S. diplomats and military leaders dealing with Iraq must be prepared for Iranian attempts to take advantage of serious disagreements between Baghdad and Riyadh after Washington withdraws its troops from Iraq. To contain Iran while supporting stability and democracy, the United States must be prepared to mediate between Saudi Arabia and Iraq and limit Iranian efforts to insert itself into such a process. Since key Saudi concerns may involve Iraqi government actions in Sunni Arab areas, the United States will have to be aware of issues in those areas, and be prepared to support measures to increase Sunni Arab willingness to participate in the political system along with a Shi'ite and Kurdish willingness to share power.

THE SAUDI-IRANIAN RIVALRY AND THE FUTURE OF MIDDLE EAST SECURITY

Introduction.

Saudi Arabia and Iran have viewed themselves as serious rivals for influence in the Middle East, particularly the Gulf area, at least since Iran's 1979 Islamic Revolution and the 1980-88 Iran-Iraq War, when Riyadh provided strong diplomatic and financial backing to Baghdad. The nature of this rivalry has a fluctuated significantly in the decades since Iran's Islamic Revolution, and the rivalry approached the level of a cold war in the years immediately following the ouster of the last Iranian shah by Islamic revolutionaries. In more recent years, limited cooperation between these two states has been possible within an overall atmosphere of suspicion and competition. Yet, even at high points in this relationship, cooperation between these two states is almost always tinged with suspicion. Additionally, in 2011, the Saudi-Iranian relationship took a dramatic turn for the worse due to strong disagreements over the wave of unrest known as the Arab Spring and the March 2011 Saudi-led military intervention to prop up the Bahraini monarchy.

Rivalry between the two states is often fueled by significant ideological and geopolitical differences that can become more divisive during times of regional turbulence. Saudi Arabia is governed by a Sunni Muslim absolute monarchy with a political agenda that often centers on preserving the status quo in the Gulf region. The Saudi leadership works closely with the smaller Gulf Arab monarchies to achieve this objective, sometimes assuming the role of a well-intentioned, if somewhat overbearing, "older brother."[1]

1

This coordination is frequently carried out through the Gulf Cooperation Council (GCC), a six-nation regional organization consisting entirely of Gulf Arab monarchies and based in Riyadh.[2] As part of its long established traditionalist orientation, the Saudi leadership is uncomfortable with the idea of expanding regional democracy, and often looks with concern on the possibility that Arab monarchies or other conservative states will be replaced by radical, liberal, or populist governments. The Saudi Royal Family is unwilling to share power with elected bodies in their own country and has sought to pressure other monarchies to reject this option and thereby avoid setting what Riyadh views as the wrong kind of example.[3] Conversely, Iran seldom seeks to defend the regional status quo regarding pro-Western monarchies, although it maintains an uneven level of commitment to revolutionary changes throughout the Middle East. This commitment is usually based on prevailing regional conditions and the degree to which potential change in various Middle Eastern countries appears to benefit Tehran. Another factor influencing Iranian foreign policy is the existence of ongoing power struggles in Tehran where different leaders often work at cross purposes for a variety of reasons including efforts to outmaneuver and weaken their political rivals. Iran is a non-Arab and non-Sunni country, and these factors are important in Iranian interaction with Saudi Arabia and other Arab states. As a general principle, Tehran also seeks to eliminate U.S. influence in the region, although Iranian leaders can sometimes see some limited value to U.S. regional diplomacy on those few occasions where Iranian and U.S. interests overlap to some extent.

Sectarian issues often influence the policy orientations of both states. Saudi Arabia has never been known for its strong commitment to religious diversity even within the Islamic community. Rather, Saudi Arabian society mostly embraces the ultra-conservative form of Islam usually known in the West as Wahhabism, although its adherents usually prefer the terms Unitarians or Salafis.[4] According to Thomas Hegghammer, a scholar of political Islam, mainstream Saudi religious scholars often did not view non-Wahhabis to be Muslims throughout the kingdom's early history. This approach changed in the 1950s when the Saudi Grand Mufti met with senior non-Wahhabi religious leaders of Sunni Arab communities outside of Saudi Arabia.[5] Despite this breakthrough, Saudi views of Shi'ite Muslims often remained disapproving into contemporary times. Saudi Arabia is therefore often described as hostile to Shi'ite empowerment throughout the region, and concerned that its own Shi'ite minority of two million people could emerge as a source of recurring difficulties for the government.[6] Iranian leaders, by contrast, often tend to be publicly dismissive of the divide between Sunnis and Shi'ites, but their consistent support for Shi'ite parties to any dispute suggests a deeper commitment to the members of their own sect. Iran often views itself as the chief defender of Shi'ite rights, although it does not consider this to be its only important regional role. Rather, Iranian leaders often view their country as a key regional state that stands as an important leader for the Islamic World.

Despite their competition with Riyadh, the Iranians most serious military rival for influence within the region is the United States, not Saudi Arabia. Correspondingly, Tehran often finds itself in the difficult position of opposing Saudi foreign policy objectives while seeking to avoid pushing the United States and Saudi Arabia into a closer political relationship. In this

3

environment, major Iranian leaders have often found it necessary to reassure the Saudis in public that they do not wish them ill.[7] Rather, they maintain that the United States is seeking to "dupe" the Gulf States into believing that the Islamic Republic constitutes a threat when it does not.[8] In some ways, the competition between Iran and the GCC states mirrors that of the United States with Iran, while in other ways these rivalries differ. Both regional leaderships are aware of ways in which they can seek advantages by maintaining a civil dialogue with the other party when this is possible. The Iranians are often at odds with Saudi Arabia and its allies, but sometimes seek to project that opposition in ways that focus most of their criticism on the United States. Conversely, Saudi Arabia remains alert to the danger that an assertive opposition to Iran could cause Tehran to escalate its acts of hostility. At various points in the relationship, Riyadh has even provided reassuring comments about Iran's peaceful intensions and high level visits have occurred between the two countries.

Additionally, neither Tehran nor Riyadh is immune to the political turbulence now sweeping the Middle East. Saudi Arabia has seen limited levels of political discontent during the Arab Spring, while Iran experienced serious unrest in 2009 following its disputed June presidential election, which is widely understood to have been "stolen" by the Ahmadinejad government.[9] Saudi Arabia seems to have contained serious domestic unrest by introducing massive new economic benefits programs for its citizens designed to increase their stake in the current political system. Iran, by contrast, used repression to defeat the Green Movement, which called for substantial reform and the decertification of President Ahmadinejad's dis-

4

puted re-election victory in the immediate aftermath of the 2009 election crisis. To the extent possible, both countries will correspondingly adjust their foreign and domestic policies to guarantee regime survival in the face of regional unrest. The future replacement of either or both countries' governments, should this occur, will probably alter rather than eliminate their rivalry, which is based on a variety of factors in addition to the differing systems of government.

The Background of Saudi-Iranian Relations.

Iran's 1979 Islamic revolution overthrew a pro-American autocrat and replaced his government with a radical Islamic regime to the consternation of both the United States and Saudi Arabia. After achieving power, the Iranian revolutionaries quickly established themselves in strong opposition to both the institution of monarchy (which they had just ended in their own country) and the pro-American foreign policy of Saudi Arabia and the smaller Gulf Arab states.[10] In November 1979, shortly after the success of the Iranian revolution, serious unrest ignited among Shi'ites in Saudi Arabia's Eastern Province, beginning with an illegal religious procession to celebrate the important Shi'ite holiday of Ashura. These religious activities had a political edge to them, and some members of the crowd carried pictures of the Iranian revolutionary leader, Ayatollah Ruhollah Khomeini, as well as signs denouncing the Saudi government and United States. When Saudi authorities attempted to disperse the crowds, three days of rioting ensued, culminating in considerable property damage. The Saudi Arabian National Guard (SANG) was then called upon to suppress the riots, which it did with a number of civilian

5

casualties.[11] Riyadh viewed Iran as the instigator of these problems.

In the early zealous years following the Islamic Revolution, Tehran directed a great deal of incendiary propaganda against the Saudis and what the Iranians called Riyadh's American brand of Islam. Adding to the discord, during the early 1980s, Iranian pilgrims repeatedly disrupted the Hajj pilgrimage to Mecca in Saudi Arabia which all Muslims who are able must make at least once in their lifetime.[12] This problem became a crisis in 1987 when Iranian protest efforts led to over 400 people being killed as demonstrations turned into riots.[13] Iran blamed Saudi Arabia for the incident and in a sea of invective demanded that Riyadh turn over custody of the Holy Places to the Islamic Republic.[14] Saudi Arabia, which closely controls the entry of foreigners into the kingdom, had few options other than accepting at least some Iranian Muslims seeking to fulfill a religious duty, but Riyadh also moved to dramatically reduce the number of Iranians allowed into the kingdom for Hajj in the aftermath of this event. After Ayatollah Khomeini's death in 1989, relations gradually improved between Saudi Arabia and Iran, with post-Khomeini leaders including Ali Akbar Hashemi Rafsanjani and Mohammad Khatami, who established themselves as less contentious than their predecessor. Khatami, in particular, sought to improve relations with Riyadh and end Iranian subversion and covert action directed against Saudi Arabia.[15] In 1999, he became the first serving Iranian president to visit Saudi Arabia, where he was courteously received. Nevertheless, neither Rafsanjani nor Khatami were fully able to control the hard liners, and the Islamic Revolutionary Guards Corps (IRGC) remained capable of conducting covert actions in foreign countries, including Saudi Arabia, without consulting the president, who was not their commander-in-chief (the Supreme Leader is constitutionally at the top of the IRGC chain of command). Since 1989 the office of Supreme Leader has been held by Ayatollah Ali Khamenei who is conservative and suspicious of reform.

President Khatami's effort to improve relations with Saudi Arabia was further motivated by occasional U.S. efforts to persuade the Gulf States to increase their role in isolating Iran due to that country's support for terrorism and suspicions about a surreptitious Iranian nuclear weapons program. U.S. diplomatic efforts have increased as concerns about that program have grown over time, while Khatami's successor as president, Mahmoud Ahmadinejad, has not made improving relations with Riyadh a priority. This failure seems to have led to predictable results. In early 2010, then-Secretary of Defense Robert Gates and Secretary of State Hillary Clinton called for the Gulf Arab states to use their influence with China to help persuade Beijing to agree to tough United Nations (UN) Security Council sanctions on Iran. Saudi Arabia, for its part, appeared publicly skeptical that increased sanctions would slow the Iranian nuclear program and displayed no public interest in approaching China on this issue.[16] Privately things might have been different, and various journalist sources suggested that Foreign Minister Prince Saud made a confidential effort to encourage China to support sanctions.[17] Secretary of Defense Gates also stated, without elaborating, that he had detected an increased Saudi willingness to use its commercial ties with China to push Beijing to distance itself from Iran.[18] In any event, the Chinese agreed to a fourth round of UN sanctions, including a comprehensive arms embargo that passed the Security Council in June 2010. There remained limits to the level of Chinese support for efforts to sanction Iran, and Beijing later criticized President Barack Obama for signing a bill that imposed more expansive unilateral American sanctions.[19]

These events are not unusual. Riyadh has often found itself navigating between U.S. policy priorities and maintaining some level of normal relations with Tehran. No one in Riyadh wishes to return to the poisoned relations of the early 1980s when Iran was intensely involved in supporting propaganda, subversion, and terrorism directed at the Arab monarchies. Likewise, the Saudis and other GCC states do not wish to place themselves in a position where they are automatically brought into an escalating political conflict or even a war between the United States and Iran, should one break out. Beyond the gamesmanship, however, issues do matter, and the Iranian nuclear program is of considerable concern to the Saudis.[20] Should Tehran cross the nuclear threshold, this development could add enormously to Iran's regional standing and the prestige of the Islamic Revolution. The damage to the Iranian nuclear infrastructure caused by the Stuxnet computer virus/worm has been described as serious by a variety of journalist sources, but it is unclear how long such assaults will delay the acquisition of an Iranian nuclear weapon. It is also unclear if the Iranian discovery of a second major computer virus attack following the Stuxnet strike is a real event, and, if so, if it is a serious and potentially debilitating attack.[21] Moreover, a nuclear armed Iran is often viewed as having a much more robust capability to threaten or engage in either unconventional or conventional military operations since other states may be more reluctant to escalate any confrontation with a nuclear power. Additionally, friendly Arab states might fear that U.S. backing for any disagreement with Tehran would be less enthusiastic, should Iran become a nuclear power.

Riyadh and Tehran View Egypt and the Arab Spring.

The 2011 wave of pro-democracy and anti-regime protests known as the Arab Spring introduced new concerns for both Saudi Arabia and Iran within the framework of their regional priorities. Neither government's vital interests were involved in the outcome of the struggle in Tunisia where the Arab Spring began, but both leaderships became especially interested in these events once the unrest spread to Egypt. President Hosni Mubarak's Egypt had sometimes played a significant role in opposing the expansion of Iranian influence in the Middle East, and the two countries never re-established diplomatic relations throughout the years of the Mubarak presidency. In particular, Mubarak often worked against the interests of the radical Palestinian Islamist group Hamas, which is an important and well-funded ally of Tehran. The future of Egyptian-Iranian relations consequently remains uncertain, as Egyptians decide on their future foreign policy orientations and priorities following the revolution. There is, nevertheless, a strong bias among Egyptians favoring a dramatically expanded regional leadership role for their country after the long years of a mostly passive foreign policy under Mubarak.[22] Simultaneously, the interim military government has been under public pressure to improve its relations with the Palestinians, including Hamas. In late May 2011, Egypt opened its border with the Gaza Strip to ease the Israeli blockade of that territory, which was

9

imposed after Hamas seized control of Gaza. Egyptian leaders announced the Fatah/Hamas reconciliation rendered the blockade unnecessary, a very different interpretation of the situation than found in Israel. Egyptian Foreign Minister Nabil al-Arabi stated that his country's previous involvement with the blockade was "shameful."[23]

In the short term, the ouster of a hostile Egyptian president following an 18-day uprising may play to Iranian advantage, although in the long term there could be problems for Tehran. Currently, Egypt's future governance is subject to considerable uncertainty, and the Iranians are calling for an Islamist government, which, at this point, could only be led by the Muslim Brotherhood, Egypt's most important contemporary Islamist movement. While Iranian preferences are irrelevant for Egyptian priorities, the destruction of the Mubarak regime is expected to allow Egypt's Muslim Brotherhood a chance to compete for a share of political power. If this organization rises to political dominance in Egypt, the United States may face a potentially dramatic setback, but this sort of development would not necessarily be advantageous to Tehran. Ideological regimes can often emerge as bitter rivals, which viciously denounce each other for failing to understand and implement the correct path. The potential for such developments have already been seen elsewhere in the Middle East, including Kuwait, where hardline Sunni Islamists are often among Iran's most bitter critics.[24] In the Kuwaiti parliament, for example, various Sunni Islamist leaders do little to hide their deep hostility toward the Iranians, which is clearly influenced by their strongly sectarian outlook.[25] In this spirit, some opposition Kuwaiti members of parliament (MPs) have sharply criticized their

Prime Minister for failing to support Saudi Arabia by dispatching Kuwaiti troops to Bahrain in March 2011 to help crush Shi'ite-led demonstrations.[26] Additionally, the decision for a large and important country like Egypt to play a more important regional role might inevitably place it in disagreement with Iran, which seeks a similar position of leadership.

Despite these potential difficulties between Cairo and Tehran, the Saudi leadership also has trepidations over Egyptian developments, and now considers their kingdom to be more isolated in efforts to contain Iranian influence without Mubarak's Egypt.[27] The Riyadh leadership viewed the Egyptian uprising with considerable alarm once it started gathering momentum and quickly and severely began criticizing the protesters while proclaiming solidarity with Mubarak. At the beginning of the crisis, Saudi King Abdullah condemned what he called protester acts of "malicious upheaval" and *fitnah* (creating discord and chaos within the Islamic community).[28] Later, as the Saudis understood the increased likelihood that the Mubarak regime would be ousted, they softened their rhetoric and focused on calling for a peaceful settlement between the government and its opponents.[29] In the aftermath of Mubarak's fall, it seems increasingly possible that Riyadh will become more engaged in regional politics since it is no longer certain that it can depend upon Egypt to play a major role in supporting the containment of Iran.

While Saudi Arabia watched the Mubarak ouster with horror, the Iranian leadership also saw some potential opportunities. Early in the crisis, Iranian Supreme Leader Ayatollah Ali Khamenei made enthusiastic statements endorsing the Egyptian protesters and attempting to portray events in that country as an

Iranian-style revolution likely to lead to an Egyptian Islamic republic.[30] He further stated that region-wide regime-changing upheaval and demands for Islamic government were natural extensions of Iran's 1979 Revolution. This set of statements represents an unlikely analysis of events since Islamic elements were not leading either the Tunisian or Egyptian revolutions, although such groups did hope to benefit from the revolutionary aftermath. Khamenei's statements are more objectively understood to represent good politics, suggesting that populations in both countries sought to oust their leaders in order to install an Islamic government based on the Iranian model. Iranians, by contrast, already have an Islamic republic, and under this logic there is no need to challenge the Tehran government with grievances such as those directed at Mubarak's regime. Khamenei has also publicly worried that the United States will "confiscate" the Arab Spring revolutions.[31]

Following Mubarak's removal from power, the Tehran leadership requested that Egypt take the "courageous step" of reestablishing diplomatic relations with Iran.[32] Then-Egyptian Foreign Minister Nabil al-Arabi seemed well-disposed to this action and stated in April 2011 that, "The Egyptian and Iranian people deserve relations which reflect their history and civilization, provided they are based on mutual respect of state sovereignty and non-interference in any kind of internal affairs."[33] Predictably, Riyadh reacted with shock to these overtures and shortly after al-Arabi's statement pressed Egypt to limit any rapprochement with Iran, noting a surge in hostility between Tehran and the GCC states following the March 2011 Saudi intervention in Bahrain. In late April 2011, Egyptian Prime Minister Essam Sharaf met with Saudi King

Abdullah in Riyadh for comprehensive discussions of key regional issues where the king clearly emphasized GCC concerns about Iran. In response, Prime Minister Sharaf stressed Egypt's interest in "stronger political relations" with Saudi Arabia, as well as the need to "bolster economic cooperation."[34] Riyadh's decision in late May 2011 to grant Egypt $4 billion in loans and grants quickly became a powerful incentive to respect Saudi priorities, especially in light of Egypt's declining tourism revenues and the interruption of Western private investment in the Egyptian economy.[35] Additionally, some of the smaller Gulf Arab states, especially Qatar, appear to be interested in helping Egypt with loans and grants as well.[36] While the Qataris have better relations with Iran than Saudi Arabia, they would likely still be concerned if Cairo moved too rapidly to improve relations with Tehran.

Currently, both Iran and Saudi Arabia remain uncertain over how Egypt's foreign policy fundamentals might evolve, and both are encouraging Cairo to move more closely in line with them. The Arab Spring also introduces the possibility that various other governments beyond Egypt, Tunisia, and Libya may be overthrown, creating gaps that can be exploited by a variety of nations who may attempt to realign post-revolutionary governments or take advantage of chaos. Saudi Arabian and the smaller Gulf Arab states are particularly concerned about preventing the overthrow of any monarchical Arab government. To this end, the GCC has shown an interest in offering full membership to the two Arab monarchies that are not yet part of the organization, Jordan and Morocco.[37] Such membership can be lucrative, and the extending of invitations for Jordan and Morocco to apply for membership reflects a concern by current GCC members to bolster monarchies that do not have much wealth, even though they are not geographically part of the Gulf.

Saudi-Iranian Competition in the Gulf Area.

The most important arena of Saudi-Iranian conflict traditionally has been the Gulf, although this competition has recently expanded to include efforts to influence post-Saddam Iraq. In the struggle for Gulf influence, Saudi Arabia has consistently maintained a higher level of political influence with local states than Iran. Riyadh has worked diligently to establish strong ties with the other Gulf monarchies and with Yemen in order to support regional stability. The GCC, which includes the six Gulf monarchies, was established in 1981 during the Iran-Iraq War as part of a strategy for these countries to advance their common interests in the face of regional turmoil. Since that time, the GCC has developed into a useful instrument for advancing its members' conservative approach to regional security. Likewise, Saudi Arabia is more influential in Yemen than any other regional or extra-regional power due to its willingness to commit impressive financial resources to the Yemeni economy, even in times of political upheaval.[38]

While Iran cannot hope to compete with Saudi regional clout in the Gulf, it does seek to influence Gulf Arab states, and is especially interested in pressuring them to minimize or eliminate their military links to the West. Tehran also seeks to establish some degree of influence with local Arab Shi'ite communities in order to pressure the Gulf Arab governments on issues of particular importance to Tehran. The GCC does not have a unified strategy to deal with the expansion of

Iranian power, although each of the Gulf Arab leaderships is concerned about Iranian assertiveness to varying degrees.[39] In particular, some states view Tehran as having the power to inspire and support internal opposition to their governments. Gulf nations with a significant number of Shi'ites often view themselves as particularly vulnerable to Iranian subversion since Shi'ite communities are often considered more susceptible to Iranian propaganda than Sunni Muslims. The Bahraini leadership has been especially concerned since it maintains a Sunni monarchy and a majority Shi'ite population in a country where relations between the two communities have experienced serious episodes of violence even before the dramatic events of the Arab Spring.[40] In 1994-99, for instance, there was an especially serious cycle of violence, confrontations, and repression between opposition Shi'ites and the monarchy.[41]

The above concerns are informed by some recent history. Middle Eastern Sunni-Shi'ite tensions in the recent past have often been at least partially linked to the state of relations between Iran and the Arab World. The most important example of this trend was the 1979 Iranian Revolution, which was viewed by some Arab Shi'ites as an empowering event.[42] According to Yitzhak Nakash, a leading scholar of Shi'ite politics, Saudi Arabian Shi'ites regard the era following the Iranian revolution as the most difficult in their recent history because of increased Saudi government suspicion and repression, as well as the escalating hostile rhetoric of Saudi Arabia's government-supported Sunni clerics.[43] Moreover, increased government repression helped to render the Saudi Shi'ites more receptive to Iranian propaganda. Formal reconciliation between the Saudi government and Shi'ite community leaders occurred in 1993, but bitterness and continuing anti-Shi'ite discrimination remain, albeit at lower levels.[44] Tensions also increased in some Gulf Arab countries during the Iran-Iraq War, when many Shi'ites were viewed as potentially sympathetic to Iran's efforts to encourage armed opposition to anti-Iranian Sunni monarchies.[45]

Sunni-Shi'ite tensions have been especially worrisome in Kuwait. Kuwait has a population which is around 30-40 percent Shi'ite, and some of the Shi'ite leadership has claimed their community faces ongoing problems with discrimination. An especially unfortunate time occurred during the Iran-Iraq War of 1980-88, when a small but serious campaign of Shi'ite terrorism was directed against the government for supporting Iraq in the struggle against Iran, a decision the Kuwaiti government later came to regret.[46] More recently, Kuwaiti leaders and media have expressed occasional concerns about Iranian sleeper agents, whom the Iranians could activate to perform acts of sabotage in any future conflict involving Kuwait or U.S. military bases there.[47] On at least one occasion, the authorities have arrested individuals whom they have described as members of an Iranian espionage and covert action ring.[48] In March 2011, two Iranians and a Kuwaiti national were convicted in a Kuwaiti court of espionage on behalf of Iran and sentenced to death.[49] The charges centered on accusations that the suspects had obtained information on the Kuwaiti military and U.S. military units in Kuwait, and then passed it on to the Iranian Revolutionary Guards Corps.[50] In explaining the meaning of the trial, one Kuwaiti columnist stated that "Iran is shown to be systematically enlisting people to spy on its behalf."[51] Kuwait also expelled Iranian diplomats for espionage activities and recalled the Kuwaiti ambassador from Tehran as part of the fallout from the crisis.[52] The Iranians, for their part, have denied the existence of spy rings in Kuwait and accused the United States of pressuring the GCC states to accuse Iran of interfering in their domestic politics.[53]

Saudi Arabia and Iran have also maintained serious differences over the recent conflict between the Yemeni government and Yemen's Houthi minority, who live in Sa'ada province in the northern part of that country. Both Saudi and Yemeni government leaders have frequently accused Iran of backing the Houthi rebels with funding, training, and material aid. Yemen further claims that such support is provided either directly by Iran or through Arabic speaking surrogates such as the radical Lebanese group, Hezbollah.[54] Yemen's charges involving Iranian materiel support and training have not been proven and may be at least partially based on the fact that the rebels are Shi'ite, although they are Fiver Shi'ites rather than the Twelver Shi'ites found in Iran. The Iranian leadership adds to this perception with rhetorical support for the Houthis in a policy of religious solidarity, but it is difficult to imagine they could remain silent on an issue so important to the Shi'ite community.[55] Saudi and Yemeni government officials have sometimes charged that the Houthi leadership seeks to move its followers away from the principles and practices of moderate Shi'ite Islam to a more militant form of Twelver Shi'ism modeled after the Iranian approach to religion.[56]

The Yemeni government's conflict with the Houthis assumed a new dimension with direct Saudi Arabian military intervention into the northern Yemen in November 2009. At this time, some of the rebels crossed into Saudi territory, killing at least two border guards and apparently taking control of two or more Saudi border villages.[57] These audacious actions provoked a strong Saudi response due to the Riyadh leadership's anger over the aggressive violation of its sovereignty and the special concerns they maintain about hostile forces based in Yemen. Yemen has a 700-mile border with Saudi Arabia that is porous in many places and can be used by criminals, smugglers, terrorists, and insurgents. The easy availability of arms in Yemen is a further complication, and most of the illegal weapons and explosives smuggled into Saudi Arabia come from Yemen. The Saudis correspondingly watched the Sa'ada conflict carefully, and became especially concerned when Houthi forces crossed into Saudi territory. Houthi spokesmen stated that they had crossed into Saudi Arabia because Riyadh had allowed the Yemeni military to use their territory to wage war against them.[58] In response, Riyadh unleashed military strikes against Houthi rebels with the permission of the Sana'a government. This engagement rapidly emerged as the largest combat operation that Saudi Arabia had undertaken since the 1991 Gulf War. Saudi tactics in this conflict involved the heavy use of artillery and airpower bombardment followed by the deployment of infantry in mopping up operations.[59] The goal of this form of warfare was to destroy large elements of the Houthi forces with ordinance so that Saudi infantry could more easily defeat the residual military forces. Such tactics were only partially successful.

The Saudi army reported that at least 133 of its soldiers were killed in action, with an undisclosed number of others wounded or captured in the fighting.[60] The Saudis discontinued their military involvement in the war in February 2010, when the Houthis withdrew from Saudi territory, a cease fire involving both the Yemeni and Saudi governments was established and all Saudi prisoners were returned.[61] It remains possible that, at a time they feel most beneficial to them, the Houthis will seek to take advantage of the 2011 Yemeni crisis in governance to renew their demands for regional autonomy should government authority continue to recede.

The March 2011 Saudi-Led Intervention in Bahrain and the Iranian Response.

The island nation of Bahrain is currently an important center of Saudi-Iranian political conflict. This small state is ruled by a Sunni Royal family, and Sunni Muslims comprise the political elite of the nation, although Sunnis make up, at most, 35 percent of the population. Bahrain's close proximity to Saudi Arabia has often caused Riyadh to pay special attention to it. The Saudis are continuously suspicious of Iranian intentions regarding Bahrain, due to its majority Shi'ite population. Bahrain is also connected to Saudi Arabia by the 16-mile King Fahd causeway, and political activity there can consequently echo throughout the kingdom. The Bahraini monarchy has consistently welcomed Saudi support including financial aid and does not display the independent streak that can be seen with some of the wealthier small states of the Gulf, most notably Qatar.

Bahrain has endured a series of difficult encounters with Iran under both the last Iranian shah and the Islamic Republic, dating back to the formal independence of the Bahraini state from protectorate status under the United Kingdom (UK) in 1971. At that time, the shah revived historical Iranian claims to Bahrain and announced that the island nation would be reunited with its Iranian homeland upon the British withdrawal. He also maintained that unification would be accomplished by force if necessary. Iranian claims were nevertheless weak and based on the temporary Persian occupation of Bahrain in the 18th century.[62] Most leading members of the international community opposed such an annexation. The crisis was averted when the shah instead focused his attention on seizing three tiny but strategically important islands near the mouth of the Gulf. These islands were also claimed by the United Arab Emirates (UAE) which, like Bahrain, had achieved independence in 1971. Iran then backed away from its claim to Bahrain, but Manama's problems with Iran did not end with the overthrow of the Iranian shah. In a burst of revolutionary exuberance, Ayatollah Rouhani, a leading spokesman of the Islamic Republic, briefly reasserted the Iranian claim to Bahrain shortly after the shah's removal from power, although his irredentist statements received almost no official follow-up.[63] Also, during this time frame, Iranian naval maneuvers near Bahraini waters led to a request from Manama for Saudi Arabian military support. Riyadh met the request and airlifted two infantry brigades for temporary duty in Bahrain.[64]

Even more ominously, in December 1981, 73 Bahrainis were arrested and accused of planning a coup against the Bahraini government. This plot was unexpectedly uncovered when a Dubai airport immigration official noticed various irregularities in the passports of some young men waiting for a flight to Bahrain. These individuals and others later identified as part of their network were charged with being members of the Tehran-based Islamic Front for the Liberation of Bahrain and coordinating their subversive actions with Iranian intelligence.[65] Iran vehemently denied involvement in the effort to overthrow the government.[66] The Bahraini and Saudi leaderships remained certain that Iran was responsible for the planned coup attempt, and the entire episode helped to move Bahrain and Saudi Arabia closer to Saddam Hussein in the then-ongoing Iran-Iraq War.[67] Many Saudi and Bahraini Sunni leaders, including Bahraini King Hamid, remain deeply concerned about this history and harbor strong suspicions about Iranian designs for sovereignty over Bahrain.

Currently, almost one-third of Bahrain's Shi'ites are Arabic-speakers of Persian origin, who are often particularly distrusted by the Sunni monarchy. Even prior to the Arab Spring unrest, violent confrontations have occurred between the communities. In a variety of instances after 1981, the government claims to have unmasked additional terrorist cells linked to Iran. The government has also conducted harsh periodic campaigns to root out any actual or potential resistance in the rural Shi'ite areas.[68] The ability of the Iranians to influence the majority of Bahrain's Shi'ite citizens is nevertheless in considerable doubt. Most Bahraini Shi'ites appear to be more interested in seeking spiritual guidance from the leading Shi'ite clergy in Iraq rather than in Iran.[69] These clerical leaders, including Grand Ayatollah Ali Sistani, have a tradition of "quietism," which calls for religious leaders to confine their statements to moral and religious issues and remain outside of politics. Ayatollah Sistani's quietism nevertheless could not extend to the Bahraini revolt which began in February 2011, and he called upon the regime to stop attacking unarmed civilians.[70]

Beginning in February 2011 and continuing throughout the 2011 Bahraini mass demonstrations for expanded rights and democracy, the Saudi leadership solidly backed King Hamid, stating somewhat disingenuously that it stood "with all its power behind the state and people of Bahrain."[71] At this point, Bahraini protestors were focusing their attention on the need for political and economic reform, including efforts to address unemployment, anti-Shi'ite discrimination, severe poverty, and the powerlessness of the elected parliament.[72] These demonstrators were mostly Shi'ite, although some sympathetic Sunnis were also involved with the movement at its early stages. Later, when some of the demonstrators began calling for the end of the Khalifa monarchy, virtually all Sunni support evaporated.[73] In Riyadh, the leadership viewed either a constitutional monarchy or a republic as an anathema and feared that revolutionary actions in Bahrain would provide an unacceptable incitement for the Saudi population, as well as empowering an unpredictable Shi'ite majority that could easily collaborate with Iranian military and intelligence organizations.

As the crisis escalated, Bahraini authorities declared martial law and sought help from other Gulf monarchies in suppressing the unrest. On March 14, 2011, Saudi Arabia sent around 1,000 troops to support the Bahraini government in its effort to suppress the overwhelmingly Shi'ite protesters. Around 500 police officers were also sent from the UAE. Several other Arab Gulf States made token contributions to the effort, and all GCC members provided political backing to the operation, which was conducted under GCC aegis following a request from the Bahraini government. The Saudi and Emirati soldiers and police did not confront the demonstrators but instead took up routine duties such as infrastructure protection. This approach was implemented in order to release Bahrain troops from routine duties and allow them to be deployed to control the demonstrators. In an effort to justify the intervention, Saudi and Bahraini officials maintained that GCC forces had intervened to help protect the island country from an Iranian threat, not to become involved in Bahraini domestic politics.[74] Tehran responded with fury to both the Saudi intervention in Bahrain and the GCC efforts to blame it for the Bahraini unrest, referring to the intervention as an occupation. Iranian leaders also demanded UN intervention to "stop the killing of the people of Bahrain."[75]

On March 21, Bahraini King Hamid stated, "An external plot has been fomented for 20 to 30 years until the ground was right for subversive designs. . . . I announce today the failure of the fomented plot."[76] These charges were clearly directed primarily at Iran, but Manama also accused the Lebanese Shi'ite group Hezbollah of playing a role in fomenting civil unrest.[77] The Bahraini government was particularly angered by a statement from Hezbollah Secretary-General Hassan Nasrallah, in which he told Bahraini demonstrators that their blood would "defeat the tyrants."[78] The Manama government suspended flights from Bahrain to Lebanon and later accused Hezbollah of training Bahraini oppositionists at military camps in Lebanon and Iran.[79] These charges remain unproven and farfetched. A departure date for the Saudi troops in Bahrain has not been announced, and it is possible that they will remain for some time. If Bahraini unrest escalates again, it is also likely that Riyadh will reinforce its troops there and even consider using them to assist Bahraini forces in suppressing riots and demonstrations. Despite GCC fulminations, no clear evidence of an Iranian covert or military role in this unrest has been made public.

Following the Saudi-led intervention, Bahraini authorities unleashed a more comprehensive crackdown. The government moved to establish its own control of all mosques throughout the country, asserting that this was necessary to ensure clerics did not promote radical ideas.[80] As part of this confrontation, the authorities destroyed at least 30 Shi'ite places of worship, including at least 16 mosques, which they claimed had been built on private or government land.[81] Whatever the merits of these charges, they were not fairly adjudicated in court, and the destruction certainly contributed to the deepening of the sectarian divide. Bahraini Sunni hostility to Shi'ites became especially overt and ugly at this time. Throughout the Bahraini demonstrations and upheaval, Sunni leaders frequently accused Shi'ites of being loyal to Iran, suggesting that they immigrate to that country. Some moderate Shi'ites admitted that community relations are harmed by the rhetoric of Shi'ite extremists, as well as the history of discrimination the Shi'ite community has suffered. Many Bahraini Sunnis also claim that Iraq's post-2003 history of internal Sunni-Shi'ite war and crisis suggests that democracy does not work in sectarian states such as their country.

There were other problematic ways in which the Bahraini government sought to consolidate its power after the Saudi-led intervention. In April 2011, the Bahraini government moved to have the Wafaq party and the Islamic Action Association, a smaller Shi'ite party, banned.[82] Wafaq is the largest political party in Bahrain and held 18 of the 40 seats in the lower (elected) house of the Bahraini parliament when unrest broke out on February 14. While the government move to crush Shi'ite political representation was almost certainly viewed with approval by Saudis, the United States reacted with concern and defended the organizations as legitimate political parties that were struggling for reform by legal means.[83] The Bahraini government quickly reconsidered its position due to sharp U.S. criticism, and movement towards outlawing these parties seems to have halted. In this regard, the Bahraini government continues to value good relations with the United States, even though its most important ally remains Saudi Arabia. It is probable that Bahrain's monarchy would like some sort of counterweight to Saudi influence in order to prevent their further decline into complete satellite status. Additionally, the Bahrainis may value U.S. cooperation against Iran and view the presence of the U.S. Fifth Fleet headquarters in Bahrain as an important deterrent in limiting Iran's military options against them.

Charges and countercharges over Bahrain also led to a substantial escalation of hostile rhetoric between Iran and the GCC over other issues. In April 2011, a meeting of the GCC foreign ministers issued a statement that the member states of the organization were "deeply worried about continuing Iranian meddling" and maintained that Tehran was "violating the sovereignty" of GCC states.[84] Previously, Riyadh had responded to Iranian criticism of the Saudi-led intervention in Bahrain by stating that Iranian charges were "irresponsible" and contained "void allegations and blatant offence against the Kingdom of Saudi Arabia."[85] Kuwaiti Foreign Minister Mohammad Sabah al-Sabah also called on Iran to change its behavior, but none of the Gulf States severed relations with Tehran.[86] Bahrain has, on a variety of occasions, arrested individuals suspected of working with Iran. In one recent incident, Bahraini authorities placed two Iranians and one Bahraini on trial on charges of conducting espionage on behalf of the Iranian Revolutionary Guards Corps.[87]

Saudi Arabia and the Syrian-Iranian Relationship.

Iran's closest Arab ally has been Syria, and Tehran has been watching the 2011 popular unrest in Syria with considerable concern. The scope of the Syrian unrest and bravery of the demonstrators is impressive, but at the time of this writing, it remains unclear whether the Assad regime will fall as a result of this unrest. The Alawite minority Islamic sect who comprise the Syrian leadership view remaining in power as essential to their future welfare and perhaps the future survival of many members of their community. Although members of the Alawite community comprise only around 10 percent of the Syrian population, the repressive regime that they dominate has remained in power for 40 years and under two presidential regimes. Elite units including Syria's Republican Guard and the 4th Armored Division are manned almost exclusively by Alawite officers and soldiers. Intelligence and security forces are also Alawite-dominated, and non-elite units usually have Alawite officers placed in key positions throughout their organizational structure. All of these structural precautions make it exceedingly difficult to mount an effective rebellion against regime authority, although angry demonstrators are certainly showing a stunning level of courage in confronting regime forces, perhaps in the hope that they can incite Sunni members of the armed forces to commit mutiny and join them.

In watching the ongoing struggle in Syria, the Tehran leadership likely understands that it has a great deal to lose. Iran and Syria have maintained good relations for over 3 decades, since the establishment of the Islamic Republic.[88] After the triumph of the Iranian Revolution, Syria was one of only two Arab states that provided diplomatic and rhetorical support for Tehran during the Iran-Iraq War (the other being Colonel Qadhafi's Libya).[89] The animosity that both Iran and Syria held for Saddam Hussein's Iraq helped to maintain this alignment, despite the very different political systems that these countries maintain. Syria, as a secular Ba'athist state, differed sharply in governmental structure from the Islamic Republic. Yet, the good relations between these states lasted beyond the Iran-Iraq War for a number of reasons. One particularly important factor in bolstering the ongoing relationship was Iran's professed willingness to provide support for Syria in any future confrontation with Israel. Both states are also deeply distrustful of the United States. During the presidency of George W. Bush, Iran and Syria were pushed together by the unrelenting hostility of the United States toward both countries. While only Iran was designated an "Axis of Evil" state, Damascus was openly worried that the U.S.-led invasion of Iraq might be followed by an invasion of Syria if Iraq could be quickly pacified and turned over to a pro-Western government, as the Bush administration hoped to do.[90] Although such Syrian concern now appears to have been unfounded, it did reflect the abysmal state of U.S.-Syrian relations at that time. While U.S.-Syrian relations improved slightly during the administration of President Obama, they remained poor due to Syrian unwillingness to reduce its backing of Hamas and Hezbollah (despite promises that they would significantly reduce such support).[91] Later, relations with Washington declined even further due to U.S. sympathy for demonstrators struggling against the brutal repression of the Assad regime.

In recent years, the Syrians and the Iranians have called themselves, along with Hamas and Hezbollah, "the axis of resistance," referring to the shared willingness of these countries and organizations to confront Israel. The Iranians often seem to view themselves as the natural leaders of this coalition, while Damascus resists Tehran's efforts to push it into a junior partnership in this relationship. This struggle has sometimes been difficult since Iran is an important source of military aid for the Syrians, particularly with regard to rocket and missile technology. Tehran has also sought to help deter future Israeli attacks against Syria. At a press conference in Damascus, Iranian Vice President Mohammad Irda Rahimi stated that Iran would fight beside Syria against any aggression by Israel.[92] Damascus, by contrast, appears to have less to offer to Tehran. The chief value of the Syrian relationship to Iran is providing it with the logistical support that allows Tehran to support its allies in Lebanon. Since Hezbollah is a Syrian ally as well, it is difficult to maintain that Syria is making any sort of sacrifice to support the Iranians in this way. Additionally, Iran's value as an ally against Israel has probably diminished as the Assad regime has become increasingly aware that Israeli leaders doubt that regime change in Syria will enhance Israeli security. Interestingly, Israelis appear divided in their assessment of the implications of Syrian unrest for their country. While generally detesting the Damascus regime, the Israelis are also concerned about an energized and equally anti-Israel post-Assad regime replacing a decrepit Ba'athist government.[93]

The key questions for many Israelis may be whether a democratic revolution in Syria can produce a liberal regime, and, more importantly, could revolution in Syria help reignite revolutionary turmoil in Iran, such as what occurred in the aftermath of the disputed 2009 election.

As noted, Syrian leaders have sometimes believed that their country is or could become the junior partner in the relationship with Iran. This concern may be one of a number of reasons for Syria to establish good or at least acceptable relations with other regional powers. In pursuing this effort to gain a variety of allies, Damascus established dramatically improved relations with Turkey prior to the Arab Spring, although these relations then collapsed as Ankara became increasingly critical of escalating Syrian repression in 2011.[94] It is also a serious oversimplification to suggest that Syria has automatically sided with Iran on all major issues. In Iraqi politics, the Assad regime has consistently backed secular leader Ayad Allawi, and Damascus also maintains a friendly relationship with some deposed Iraqi Ba'athists despised by Tehran.[95] Despite this preference, the Iraqi government, including many of its Shi'ite leaders, have been generally supportive of the Syrian government throughout the popular uprising against it.[96] The chief reason for this support appears to be a fear among Iraqi Shi'ites that Assad will be succeeded by a radical Sunni regime. Such a regime might be inclined to support rebellious Sunni tribes hostile to Baghdad's Shi'ite-dominated government. The Syrians have also shown independence from Tehran on issues related to Yemen. As noted earlier, Saudi Arabia and Iran maintained deeply opposing policies on Yemen's Houthi rebellion, but, at least rhetorically, Damascus has sided with Saudi Arabia.[97] The Syrians further supported the Saudi military intervention in Bahrain in March 2011 in an especially vivid break with Tehran.[98]

As a monarchy, Saudi Arabia has maintained a long tradition of distrust towards Syria, which defines itself as a republican, and sometimes a revolutionary regime. While the Saudis have been willing to work with Syria on occasion, they do not have much in common with the Syrian state or government beyond Arabism. Since 1970, Syria has also been led by strong Alawite presidents from the Assad family. Alawites are usually viewed as a subgroup of Shi'ite Muslims that are even further from orthodox Sunni practices and beliefs than the Twelver Shi'ites found in Iran, Iraq, and Lebanon. Nevertheless, the Saudi approach of seeking to bribe and co-opt potential adversaries has been applied to Syria with considerable success on occasion, and sometimes the two nations have found the basis for serious cooperation. The most notable example of this approach may have been the 1990 Gulf crisis, when Damascus sent an armored division and supporting troops (totaling 300 tanks and 17,000 personnel) to Saudi Arabia to participate in the 1990-91 international coalition opposing Saddam Hussein's invasion of Kuwait.[99]

Saudi-Syrian relations took a dramatic turn for the worse on February 14, 2005, when former Lebanese Prime Minister Rafiq Hariri and eight of his aides died after a massive bomb placed in his car detonated as his motorcade drove home from parliament along Beirut's seafront road. In the immediate aftermath of the attack, it was almost universally assumed that the bombing was the work of the Syrian intelligence services. Saudi Arabia's special relationship with Hariri made his murder an important geostrategic setback, as well as an act of savagery directed against someone who was well-known and liked by the Saudi leadership. In the aftermath of the attack, Saudi Arabia renewed its support for UN Security Council Resolution 1559 (September 2, 2004) which required Syria to withdraw its military forces from Lebanon and backed U.S. diplomatic efforts to remove the Syrian military and intelligence services from Lebanon.[100] These efforts led to the April 2005 removal of Syrian forces from Lebanon, where they had been stationed since the mid-1970s.

At some point, the Saudis were able to overcome their hostility towards the Syrian regime, and sought to work with Damascus in an effort to help salvage a deteriorating situation in Lebanon involving political polarization aggravated by Hariri's assassination. Riyadh may also have been interested in rolling back Iranian influence in both Syria and Lebanon, while Damascus saw value in Saudi ties to avoid overdependence on Iran. In January 2010, Prince Saud stated that "If the situation reaches separation or division of Lebanon, this would mean the end of Lebanon as a model of peaceful coexistence between religions, ethnicities and different groups."[101] He went on to describe such an outcome as "a loss for the Arab nation."[102] On July 30, 2010, Assad and Saudi King Abdullah made a joint visit to Beirut to help calm the situation and defuse tensions created by the feared reaction to the expected indictment of Hezbollah members for the murder of former Prime Minister Rafiq Hariri by the UN Special Tribunal on Lebanon (STL).[103] Surprisingly, the STL did not hold Syria directly responsible for Hariri's murder, and instead issued arrest warrants for four Lebanese suspects who are Hezbollah members. Hezbollah reacted with fury to the indictment while pro-

Hariri groups demanded Lebanese cooperation with the STL. This situation has yet to be resolved, although the indicted individuals have disappeared from public view and may have fled to Iran.

More recently, both Saudi Arabia and Iran have needed to consider how Syrian unrest impacts upon their interests and how to address these new developments. Tehran clearly has the most to lose if the Assad regime is overthrown, and it is mostly standing by its Syrian ally.[104] Various U.S. and European leaders including representatives of the U.S. State Department and European Union (EU) have accused the Iranians of helping Syria repress anti-regime demonstrators, although few details of such activities have been given in public.[105] Journalistic sources suggest that Iran has provided Syria with equipment, planning advice, and technical expertise related to breaking up efforts to organize anti-government protests.[106] Some of this support may be quite useful and allow the Syrian security forces to learn from Iranian experiences in suppressing massive unrest in their country following the 2009 elections. Syrian demonstrators have also accused Iran of providing snipers to fire on the crowds in Syria, but this seems unlikely. The Syrian regime would not lack committed marksmen to perform this function, and would have little need to call upon foreigners to do so.

Iran will probably be the last country to abandon the Syrian regime for a variety of reasons, including fear of a Sunni-led successor government that will be more oriented towards working with other Arab states rather than with Iran. Tehran's leaders are also concerned about the potential emergence of a pro-American government in Damascus.[107] Either of these types of successor government may also seek a complete break from the previous relationship with Tehran. Moreover, if a new Syrian government discontinued its relationship with Iran, Tehran would lose a great deal of its capability to project power into Lebanon and perhaps the Palestinian territories, a serious setback for Iranian efforts to portray their country as a regional leader.

The uprising in Syria has also introduced a new dimension into Saudi views about Syria, which has led to a more hardline approach. This new toughness was clear when Saudi King Abdullah demanded "an end to the killing machine and the bloodshed" that the Syrian regime had unleashed against its population.[108] The Saudis, Kuwaitis, and Bahrainis also withdrew their ambassadors to Damascus in early August 2011 to protest Assad regime policies.[109] The previous détente with Damascus was significant, but Riyadh never viewed the Syrian regime as an ally, and could be expected to take some pleasure in seeing Tehran lose its most important Arab partner should this regime fall. Conversely, Riyadh almost certainly would not view the situation in Syria as an unqualified Saudi victory, even if the Assad regime was overthrown and replaced by an anti-Iranian government.[110] The Saudi leadership remains ultra-conservative, and correspondingly takes a dim view of both revolutionary turmoil and Arab democracy. A strong, vibrant Syrian democracy would at least be a serious inconvenience for Riyadh, and it could emerge as a real challenge to the Middle Eastern status quo.

Saudi-Iranian Competition in the Palestinian Territories and Lebanon.

Evaluations of Saudi Arabian attitudes and policies towards the Palestinian issue and the Middle East

Peace Process vary widely. Clearly, Riyadh is a strong supporter of Palestinian national rights and a sharp and frequent critic of Israel. Additionally, the Saudis have strongly supported Palestinian Muslim claims to East Jerusalem and are hostile to Israeli efforts to expand their presence in the old city. Critics of Saudi foreign policy sometimes charge that Riyadh tolerates or supports Palestinian terrorist activities and these concerns are examined later in this monograph. Despite the blame directed against it, a variety of observers consider the Saudi government to be moderate, or at least to have a moderate side on Arab-Israeli issues. The strongest evidence for this viewpoint is the Saudi Arabian Peace Plan adopted by the Arab League at a March 2002 summit conference in Beirut.[111] The proposal offers comprehensive recognition of Israel by all Arab League states in exchange for the return of all territories captured in the June 1967 War. Many Israeli political leaders, including Defense Minister Ehud Barak and Kadima party leader Tzipi Livni, have stated that they see many positive aspects to the Plan, although they refuse to accept it on a take-it-or-leave-it basis.[112] While Riyadh has not always been enthusiastic about the potential for progress in the peace process, Saudi leaders also fear that its complete collapse will enhance Iranian regional power at their expense. Under such conditions, the hard line approach of the Iranians would appear vindicated to many Arabs, while any efforts to negotiate peace will appear to be acquiescing to Israeli delaying tactics used to consolidate control of the Palestinian territories.

Saudi Arabia has made numerous efforts to help the Palestinians and to use its financial resources and political influence on their behalf. Riyadh maintains normal political relations with both of the major Palestinian political parties, Fatah and Hamas, the latter of which has been designated as a terrorist organization by the United States. In this regard, the Saudi government has transferred funds directly to a variety of Palestinian organizations and causes over a considerable period of time. A significant amount of this money has been provided to the Palestinian Authority in the West Bank, which is controlled by Fatah and has also been supported by the United States.[113] Financial relations with Hamas are more controversial and murky. The Saudi government has condemned terrorist actions by Hamas against the Israelis, but King Abdullah has also called Israeli military strikes into the Gaza Strip acts of genocide against the Palestinians.[114] Additionally, the Saudi government strongly maintains that it does not provide money directly to Hamas, although in the early 2000s, Saudi private money was estimated to be around half of the Hamas operating budget.[115] Since that time, both Israeli and American sources have indicated that private Saudi money flowing to Hamas has diminished or even largely dried up.[116] These developments may be the result of international pressure on Riyadh, or, more likely, Saudi discomfort that Hamas has leaned so dramatically towards Iran. It is also possible that at least some private Saudi donors have become more discrete.

Iran has approached the Palestinian problem very differently. Instead of presenting formulas for peace, Tehran has attempted to portray itself as the leading militant power supporting Palestinian rights and opposing Israel through a variety of means, including supplying weapons and funding to Palestinian Islamic militants. This leadership role is important to Tehran as a way of consolidating support for the regime internally and elevating its regional role and standing among anti-Israeli publics throughout the region. At present, Iran has clearly become the leading financial patron for Hamas. Hamas now depends so heavily on Iran that it is often accused of being a proxy. Fatah leaders have stated that Iran seeks to use Hamas to impose its own agenda on the Palestinian people.[117]

Iran's interest in providing weapons to Palestinian groups is well established. One of the most dramatic incidents involving Iranian-Palestinian relations occurred on January 3, 2002, when the Israelis captured the Palestinian owned-freighter *Karine A*. In late 2001, the *Karine A* had stopped off at an island near the Iranian coast where the ship was loaded with arms, including Katyusha rockets, mortars, Kalashnikov rifles, ammunition, anti-tank weapons, plastic explosives, and other weapons, which the Israelis maintained were to be provided to the Palestinian Authority (rather than Hamas).[118] While Iran has often been hostile to the Palestinian Authority, Tehran was interested in supporting and militarizing the al Aqsa Intifada, a Palestinian revolt against Israeli authority that broke out in September 2000. This interest in taking advantage of unfolding events seems to have been Tehran's primary motivation in seeking to provide weapons. Yassir Arafat, then the leader of the Palestinian Authority, denied any link to the ship, although he later became much more equivocal about the issue.[119] If Iran hoped to harm the peace process, it could hardly have staged a more effective undertaking. The capture of the *Karine A* also had a catastrophic impact on Israeli-Palestinian relations and undermined U.S. ties with the Palestine Authority. Unfortunately for Tehran, the *Karine A* incident also contributed to U.S. President George W. Bush's belief that Iran was an irredeemable rogue state. In his January 29, 2002, State of the Union Address, President Bush identified Iran, Iraq, and North Korea as part of an "axis of evil."

Since the *Karine A*'s capture, the success of Iranian smuggling efforts have sometimes been difficult to gauge, but a significant number of weapons have been smuggled over time to Gaza through tunnels from Egypt. The Israelis believe that many of the weapons and explosives provided in this way originate with the Iranians.[120] More dramatically, the Israelis seized an additional merchant ship in March 2011, which they reported to be loaded with missile systems as well as operating manuals in Farsi.[121] Israeli sources stated that the Iranian plan was to have these weapons offloaded in Egypt and then attempt to infiltrate them to Gaza through the tunnels. The Israelis maintain that there has been a substantial increase in problems along the Egyptian border since the January 2011 overthrow of President Mubarak.[122] Iran may seek to take advantage of this situation.

The Iranian leadership has also made a number of flamboyant but transparently hollow promises to highlight its opposition to Israel and its support of the Palestinians in response to international headlines. One such incident occurred after a Turkish aid ship was intercepted in June 2010 by the Israeli Navy, creating a major international incident including nine Turkish deaths.[123] In the aftermath of the strike, a representative of Supreme Leader Ayatollah Ali Khamenei stated that Iran's Revolutionary Guard Corps would be willing to provide naval units to escort ships bringing supplies to Gaza in the future even though Iran's ability to implement this policy was nonexistent.[124] It is difficult to believe that even the most hard line Iranian leader believes that such actions would turn out well for them, and these statements are probably best understood as propagandistic bombast.

Elsewhere in the Levant, Iran often seems to dominate the rivalry with Saudi Arabia in Lebanon. Lebanon is a small, weak state influenced by a variety of countries from both within the region and globally. In recent years, the most important powers influencing Lebanon have been Syria, Iran, the United States, Israel, and Saudi Arabia. In this struggle, Iran has some clear advantages in the competition for influence, the most important of which are its strong ties to the Lebanese political organization Hezbollah, which maintains its own militia and is known to practice terrorism.[125] Hezbollah is often identified in the West as a terrorist organization, but it is also one of the most powerful political organizations in Lebanese politics. Hezbollah operates an extensive welfare and educational network for Lebanese Shi'ites who are expected to reward the organization with their loyalty and support. Hezbollah also has its own television station (*al-Manar* television) and has consistently maintained representatives in the parliament and cabinet. Perhaps most importantly, Hezbollah is the only Lebanese political organization that currently retains a militia from the civil war era. Other political parties that used armed axillaries in the Lebanese Civil War (1975-90) have since disbanded them under the September 1989 Taif Agreement that ended that conflict. Hezbollah's decision to retain a military arm is often considered a problem by other Lebanese, although Hezbollah members and the Iranians justify such actions as a deterrent to Israeli military action.[126]

Iranian influence over Hezbollah is maintained through lavish financial and material aid, usually funneled into Lebanon through Syria.[127] Hezbollah may also be growing in its role as a strategic asset for Iran. In October 2010, Hezbollah leader Hassan Nasrallah claimed that his organization had increased its missile stocks to around 40,000 rockets and missiles, while in the 2006 War it only had around 14,000 to 20,000, of which at least 14,000 were short-range Katyusha rockets.[128] In April 2010, Israeli President Shimon Peres charged that Syria was providing SCUD missiles to Hezbollah, which would have been done in coordination with Iran. Peres was the first of a number of Israeli officials to make such charges, with U.S. journalistic sources reporting that Hezbollah has up to 10 SCUD-D missiles.[129] The International Crisis Group also suggested that Israel may have come close to attacking these weapons, according to interviews they conducted with Israeli officials.[130] Hezbollah officials refuse to discuss whether or not they had obtained such systems or anti-aircraft missiles capable of seriously increasing the threat to Israeli aircraft in a future attack.[131] As long as these weapons continue to exist, Iran will have the ability to demand that Hezbollah unleash them in any future Israeli-Iranian conflict, particularly an Israeli attack on Iranian nuclear facilities.

Saudi Arabia became especially important in Lebanese politics after it helped broker the 1989 Taif Accords, which ended the Lebanese Civil War. Following the Taif Accords, Saudi Arabia also began playing a major role in Lebanese reconstruction. In 1992, pro-Saudi Lebanese billionaire Rafiq al-Hariri became prime minister as a result of the Taif Accords leading to a clear boost of Saudi influence within Lebanon and a strong potential for Saudi involvement in economic rebuilding. Hariri, a Sunni Muslim who made his vast fortune in Saudi Arabia, quickly overshadowed the traditional Sunni elite in Lebanon because of his financial power and his close relationship with the Saudi leadership. According to Beirut's *Daily Star* editor, Michael Young, it was often difficult to discern where Hariri's personal fortune ended and Saudi funding began when being directed at Lebanese investments, patronage, and aid networks.[132] In Young's estimation, Hariri was something of a front man for Saudi interests in Lebanon.[133] He served as prime minister from 1992-98 and again from 2000-04.

The July-August 2006 Israeli military intervention into Lebanon against Hezbollah is sometimes considered to have created opportunities for Tehran since Israeli leaders, by their own admission, were deeply dissatisfied with the outcome of that intervention.[134] Israel's poorly-planned 33-day war against Hezbollah in the summer of 2006 failed to meet its objectives and dramatically elevated the status and reputation of Hezbollah and its Iranian supporters due to the spirited resistance the Lebanese Shi'ite fighters displayed. Even more dramatically, Hezbollah was able to strike back against the Israelis using large numbers of Katyusha rockets and some longer-range missiles. During the 2006 Lebanon war, Saudi officials and clerics were often critical of Hezbollah's adventurism for kidnapping two Israeli soldiers and thereby igniting the conflict.[135] Saudi caution was not always appreciated by Arab publics watching these events unfold, and at least initially many Arab observers chose to embrace the narrative of brave resistance fighters struggling against Israel's high technology war machine. According to this interpretation, Iran was viewed as helping maintain the dignity of the Arab resistance, while Saudi Arabia was blaming them for inciting the Israeli strike. This narrative began to fade over time as Hezbollah leader Hassan Nasrallah was increasingly blamed for the 1,100 Lebanese deaths in the war and the $3-5 billion worth of damage to the Lebanese economy include the destruction of 10,000 homes.[136]

In the aftermath of the 2006 war, the struggle between Iran and Saudi Arabia and their Lebanese clients continued. In the deeply fragmented environment of Lebanese politics, different groups often view Iranian involvement in their country in starkly contrasting ways. Large numbers of people within Lebanon's Shi'ite community consider Iran to be an important ally that has extended considerable support to the Lebanese in resisting what they define as Israeli aggression. The March 8 Movement, a political coalition led by Hezbollah, is an important leader of this trend, which Tehran finds to be of considerable value. Iranian President Ahmadinejad made his first state visit to Lebanon in October 2010, at a time of escalating tension between Hezbollah and its rivals, as a way of highlighting Iranian-Hezbollah ties. The 2-day visit involved a trip to the southern part of the country near the Israeli border, where Iran has also built a number of roads.[137] The Iranian president viewed the visit as highly successful and was mobbed by adoring crowds.[138]

Various other groups within Lebanon view Iran as an intruder and meddler in Lebanese politics, and seek the support of Saudi Arabia as a counterweight to Tehran, at least in the realm of financial aid. The group most closely identified with this outlook is the March 14 Movement, which includes a variety of important political leaders usually drawn from the Christian and Sunni Muslim communities. Some March 14 Movement officials are quite blunt about their assessment of the relationship with Iran. Former Prime Minister Saad Hariri, the leader of the Future Movement and son of Rafiq Hariri, went so far as to state, "We in Lebanon do not accept to be an Iranian protectorate."[139] He then went on to say that, "Saudi Arabia is the biggest and first investor in Lebanon's stability. This investment is priceless. It is the basis for Lebanon's progress and economic growth."[140] Such statements were further emphasized by a variety of other pro-Saudi politicians, including former Prime Minister Fouad Siniora, who also noted that Hezbollah ignored the role of Saudi aid in rebuilding Lebanon after the 2006 war.[141] Other leaders of the Lebanese Future Movement's Parliamentary bloc have claimed that Saudi Arabia provided tremendous support to Lebanon, surpassing that of Iran after the 2006 war, including providing funds for the construction of 55,200 residential units. These statistics were quoted in an angry debate in which Future Movement leaders strongly criticized Hezbollah leader Hassan Nasrallah for thanking Iran, but not Saudi Arabia, for post-war assistance.[142] The importance of Iran in Lebanese politics has nevertheless also been acknowledged by moderates in the Lebanese government who are known to distrust Tehran. In November 2010, then-Lebanese Prime Minister Saad Hariri made an official visit to Tehran in what was described as an effort to strengthen the economic and political ties between the two countries.[143] Iran's influence is simply too sweeping for any Lebanese Prime Minister to disregard while in office.

Prime Minister Saad Hariri's government collapsed in January 2011 when Hezbollah cabinet members and their allies resigned *en mass* in order to bring the government down. They did this over disagreements about whether or not to cooperate with the UN Special Tribunal on Lebanon (STL) investigating the murder of Rafiq Hariri in 2005. The STL was then on the verge of indicting four members of Hezbollah.[144]

After Hariri's ouster, a new Lebanese government was not assembled until 5 months later, when billionaire and former Prime Minister Najib Mikati was able to gain that post with Hezbollah backing.[145] The new cabinet was dominated by Hezbollah and its allies.[146] Under these circumstances, the Saudi Arabian and Sunni Lebanese communities' hopes for obtaining some kind of justice in the murder of Rafiq Hariri suffered a considerable setback. Mikati, for his part, strongly maintained that he is an independent politician and not a Hezbollah stooge.[147] Despite these assurances, his ministers have been widely indentified as comprising one of the most pro-Syrian and pro-Iranian cabinets in Lebanese history, and the new Prime Minister is sometimes described as a close friend of Syrian President Bashar Assad.[148]

Unsurprisingly, the Mikati government has directed no serious criticism at Syria's brutal repression of demonstrators, while the Future Movement has denounced the Syrian actions as "crimes against humanity."[149] Future Movement leader Saad Hariri has called on the Mikati government to denounce the "open massacre."[150] On one particularly memorable occasion, he presented his stance as following the lead of Saudi King Abdullah's decision to denounce Syrian actions and recall the Saudi Ambassador in Damascus. Hariri stated, "There is no doubt that the historic speech yesterday of the Custodian of the Two Holy Mosques King Abdullah bin Abdul Aziz to Syria and its people came at a pivotal moment to crown the Arab stance with an honest and firm vision which issues a warning against the risks of continued violence, bloodshed, and chaos."[151]

The establishment of the Mikati government created problems for the United States, which has previously designated Hezbollah as a terrorist organization, and took a dim view of their newfound prominence within the Lebanese government. In 2010, Lebanon received around $100 million in U.S. military aid to help strengthen its security forces. The United States provided up to $800 million in funding for military and law enforcement programs since the end of 2006.[152] Following the establishment of the Mikati government, some U.S. policymakers raised questions about continuing this aid.[153] In response, the Iranian government announced that it was willing to replace the United States as Lebanon's chief source of military aid. This change is unlikely, as any serious attempt to realign defense procurement to Iran would create a severe domestic and international crisis.[154] Saudi Arabia continues to back the Lebanese opposition, particularly the leadership of Lebanon's Sunni Muslim community.

The Saudi-Iranian Rivalry and the Future of Iraq.

Iraq is of central concern to both Iran and Saudi Arabia, and prior to 2003 mutual hostility to the Saddam Hussein regime was one of the chief anxieties that these countries shared. Both Riyadh and Tehran have contended with an unfriendly Iraq at important points in their history, and both nations are concerned about the possible emergence of a hostile regime in Baghdad. Since Saddam's ousting, this problem has appeared more difficult for Riyadh than Tehran. Iran has significantly improved its relations with Iraq under a series of post-Saddam Shi'ite dominated governments, while Saudi Arabia has maintained fairly strained relations with many Iraqi leaders including Prime Minister Nouri al-Maliki. There is also the question of oil. Iraq is now beginning a serious effort to work with international oil companies to rebuild its oil infrastructure in a way that may allow it to emerge as a leading oil exporter.[155] This development could weaken Riyadh's regional and international influence over the world oil market, but would probably not be a problem for Iran since Tehran and Baghdad have similar concerns regarding oil. More ominously, the Saudis are certainly worried that any establishment of a Shi'ite-dominated government in Baghdad could create the conditions under which Iraq and Iran could join forces to organize against them in a diplomatic propaganda, and perhaps subversion effort. Even a temporary alliance of this sort could be potentially devastating for the advancement of Saudi interests throughout the region.

Iranian leaders, despite their current influence in Baghdad, remain aware that they have more to fear from a hostile re-energized Iraq than Saudi Arabia if relations sour. The legacy of the 8-year Iran-Iraq War, in which hundreds of thousands of people were killed on both sides, is particularly sobering in this regard. The presence of hundreds of thousands of disabled war veterans (*janbazan*) within Iranian society makes the war's consequences difficult to forget.[156] More tellingly, while often judged as a stalemate, the war ended on terms significantly more favorable to Baghdad than Tehran. As the war entered its final phases, the Iranians agreed to a cease-fire only after offensive operations no longer seemed possible for them. At the war's conclusion, Iraq gained control of disputed territory, and the border with Iran was defined in a way that reflected Iraqi interests.[157] Several years later, Iran watched with interest as Iraq was comprehensively defeated in Operation DESERT STORM in conventional combat. While Iranian leaders were delighted to see

Saddam defeated, it was troubling to watch U.S. forces easily slice through Iraqi military forces that they had been unable to defeat in 8 years of fighting. Currently, the Iranians with their own aging conventional weapons and equipment would not wish to be at war with an Iraq armed with Western military technology.[158] While Iran has spent considerable sums on its missile forces and nuclear enrichment program, it has badly neglected its conventional forces, which have not been modernized much since the Iran-Iraq War and are obsolete by Western standards.[159] Moreover, even if Iran chose to invest in modernizing its conventional forces, this would probably be impossible because of UN sanctions, which impose a comprehensive arms embargo on Iran due to its undeclared nuclear activities.[160] The only country that is violating this embargo in any clear way is North Korea, which cannot serve as a major military patron for conventional arms.[161]

The Iranians are further concerned about the future of a U.S. military presence in Iraq, which Tehran views as providing Washington with increased conventional options against them. Even a limited or temporary U.S. Navy or Air Force presence that does not involve ground combat troops would be problematic for the Iranians. Additionally, Tehran cannot be comfortable with the prospect of a well-armed Iraq with continuing access to U.S. military technology unless its leadership believes that Iraq will emerge as a permanent ally, which can hardly be taken for granted. Currently, the Iraqi Army remains dominated by non-mechanized infantry forces, but Baghdad is also seeking to acquire expanded armored forces and a modern air force, including F-16 fighter aircraft.[162] The Iranian Air Force, which is based on older Russian/Soviet and Chinese aircraft, could never compete with a force equipped with modern Western-supplied aircraft. Some Iraqi politicians are also calling for a large and well-equipped military, which they view as a complement to Iraq's role as an important regional power, and such comments only increase Iranian unease.[163] The dangers presented to Iran by Iraqi conventional forces will naturally be mitigated if Iran crosses the nuclear threshold, but Iran may not be able to use nuclear weapons without provoking a response from the United States.[164]

Riyadh is also known to have maintained serious reservations about the 2003 U.S.-led invasion of Iraq to oust Saddam Hussein, although these concerns were not based on a fear of expanding U.S. regional influence. While the Saudis were deeply concerned about Saddam Hussein when he was at the height of his strength and aggressiveness shortly after the Iran-Iraq War, these fears receded following Iraq's massive military defeat in 1991 and the imposition of post-war military sanctions that made it difficult for Iraq to modernize and even perform proper maintenance on its weapons and military equipment. Concurrently, the Riyadh leadership understood that a friendly government in either a democratic or undemocratic Shi'ite-led Iraq would always be elusive. One of Saudi Arabia's greatest fears after Saddam's 1991 defeat was the potential emergence of an energized, anti-Saudi Shi'ite regime in Iraq led by pro-Iranian politicians. After Operation DESERT STORM ended, Riyadh appears to have viewed Saddam as a crippled and isolated Sunni strongman who was treated with loathing by much of the world and placed under ongoing sanctions. As such, his capacity to threaten Saudi Arabia was severely limited in ways that would not constrain a hostile successor.

Tehran has been significantly more active in attempting to gain influence in Iraq than Riyadh has since 2003, in part because it was especially alarmed by the sudden rise of U.S. military power and influence in its neighboring states of Iraq and Afghanistan.[165] This Iranian effort has involved diplomacy, economic investment, covert action, and cultivating Iranian clients within the Iraqi political system including the leadership of armed militias. This approach has produced results, and Iran has emerged as a major power in domestic Iraqi politics. Iraq's Prime Minister Maliki, who is drawing on a Shi'ite domestic power base, is reluctant to offend Tehran, and has stated that strategic ties between the two nations serve the interest of both.[166] He also hosted Iranian President Ahmadinejad on an official visit to Baghdad in March 2008. This was the first visit of a serving Iranian president to Iraq. In another indication of Iranian influence, Tehran has helped to broker important agreements between competing Iraqi Shi'ite factions, including helping to establish a 2010 working relationship between Maliki and populist leader Muqtada al-Sadr to help them put together a governing Shi'ite-led coalition in the Iraqi parliament.[167] Maliki and Sadr have detested each other since at least March 2008, when Maliki ordered the Iraqi army to move against Sadr's followers in Basra in Operation CHARGE OF KNIGHTS. This confrontation resulted in a number of deaths and was a substantial setback to Sadr's bid for political influence in Iraq. It is difficult to imagine that these two sides could have reached agreement without Iranian intercession.[168] The Iranians view the Sadr Movement's influence within the Iraqi government as useful, despite its leader's erratic behavior, because Sadr is so passionately committed to a speedy withdrawal of all U.S.

forces from that country. He could also reasonably be expected to oppose all future strategic ties between the United States and Iraq, and is currently the leading Iraqi politician demanding a full U.S. withdrawal from Iraq without leaving any residual force.[169]

One of the most troubling ways in which Iran exerts its influence in Iraq is through various Shi'ite militia organizations, which engage in terrorism and military strikes against U.S. troops and Iraqis opposed to these forces. These pro-Iranian militias are sometimes called Special Groups. Iran has considerable influence with them and provides weapons and training to some of these forces through the elite Iranian Revolutionary Guards Corps' al-Quds Force.[170] In the years immediately following Saddam's removal from power, the Iranians worked closely with a number of Shi'ite Iraqi political parties and movements, including the Sadr Movement. This movement maintained its own militia, the Mahdi Army (*Jaysh al Mahdi*), which received financial aid and military supplies from Tehran. Around 2007, the Iranians appear to have de-emphasized their support for the Mahdi Army due to its reckless behavior and the inability of anyone to control it. Later, in 2008, Sadr disavowed violence against other Iraqis and ordered the Mahdi Army to disarm and become a "humanitarian group."[171] At the present time, Sadr remains in Iran and controls another militia organization, the Promised Day Brigade. The Promised Day Brigade, which has a strength of 5,000 men, is a mere shadow of the Mahdi Army, which, at its peak strength, included 60,000 militiamen.[172]

Despite his problems, Muqtada al-Sadr remains an important Iraqi political and militia leader. He controls around 40 seats in the 325-member Iraqi parliament and revels in his role as an uncompromising political leader opposing any U.S. military presence in Iraq after December 2011. To underscore his commitment, Sadr has issued a number of warnings that any U.S. troops remaining in Iraq as trainers past the December 2011 deadline for their withdrawal will become targets for his militia forces.[173] This threat was reiterated following the August 2011 Iraqi government announcement that it would open talks with the United States about some U.S. troops remaining as trainers and subsequent indications of progress in these talks.[174] Sadr also stated that, "[the Iraqi] government which agrees to them staying, even if it is for training, is a weak government."[175] Iraqi domestic politics are moving in a way that suggests it will be a severe political problem for any major non-Kurdish Iraqi leader to support an extension of a U.S. military presence remaining in that country, although Baghdad's national security needs could be well-served by such a request.

Other Iranian-supported militias in Iraq include the *Asaib al Haq* (AAH-League of the Righteous), which has about 1,000 militiamen, and the *Kata'ib Hezbollah* (Party of God Brigade). The smaller size of the Hezbollah Brigades may allow them to be more easily controlled by the Iranians. The Iranians have supplied both of these groups with increasingly effective weapons including rocket assisted exploding projectiles (RAEPs), which they use for attacks on U.S. troops.[176] Iranian weapons supplied to Special Groups have been used with considerable effectiveness against U.S. forces in Iraq, causing Defense Secretary Leon Panetta in July 2011 to comment that, "We're seeing more of these weapons coming from Iran, and they've really hurt us."[177] Yet in addition to its involvement in arming the radical militias, Iran also has a number of legitimate interests in Iraq. President Ahmadinejad visited Iraq in early March 2008, at which time a variety of trade agreements were signed providing the basis for further economic ties.[178] At this time, Iran is Iraq's largest trading partner, and the Iranians are also one of the largest investors in Iraq's construction and industrial sector.[179]

Surprisingly, Washington and Tehran also had some overlapping interests in Iraq as the United States was beginning its troop drawdown in that country. The United States supported Iraqi Prime Minister Maliki and his State of Law political coalition because he was viewed as a leader of continuity who would continue to support Iraqi self-sufficiency in internal defense. Iran also supports Maliki, whom they view as a friendly Shi'ite leader whose responsiveness to the United States will probably decline after the United States withdraws from that country. Conversely, the Saudis have often been deeply critical of the U.S. policies in Iraq, which they have viewed as pro-Shi'ite, pro-Kurdish, and anti-Sunni. Saudi leaders have also sometimes portrayed U.S. policies as playing into the hands of the Iranians.[180] Saudi leaders further dislike Maliki, and accuse him of being a sectarian figure who hinders reconciliation among Iraqi communities. At an international conference in Sharm al-Sheikh, Egypt in May 2007, King Abdullah refused to meet Maliki, whom he described as, "embodying sectarian divisions."[181] Serious differences continued, and the Iraqi government has sometimes accused Saudi Arabia of failing to stop its citizens from entering Iraq and joining the Shi'ite dominated insurgency. This was a serious charge that carried the potential to complicate or even damage Riyadh's relationship with Washington.

As noted, Riyadh has not involved itself in Iraq to nearly the extent of its Iranian rivals. Saudi Arabia got off to a slower start due to its reluctance to send diplomats to Iraq in the aftermath of the invasion of that country by U.S.-led forces. Previously, the Saudis had broken relations with Iraq in 1991 on the eve of Operation DESERT STORM, but they formally reestablished these ties in 2004. Riyadh did not, however, reopen its embassy in Iraq, citing security issues and the targeting of Arab diplomats by terrorists and insurgents. Neither Iraq nor the United States took these statements at face value, although various Arab diplomats were certainly being attacked by insurgents in this time frame. Iraq reopened its embassy in Riyadh in 2007, but relations remained tense. Conversely, the Iranians appointed an ambassador to that country in May 2006.[182] The United States has encouraged the GCC states to improve ties with Iraq and possibly to include such moves as considering allowing Iraq to join the GCC, which seems almost impossible. During an April 25, 2009, visit to Baghdad, Secretary of State Clinton expressed concern about the poor state of relations between Baghdad and Riyadh according to journalistic sources, citing conversations with U.S. diplomats.[183] In a 2009 address to Arab military officers in Washington, Defense Secretary Gates stated, "The embrace of Iraq by its fellow Gulf States will help to contain the ambitions of Iran."[184]

During the lead up to the March 2010 Iraqi national election, the Saudis clearly favored secular Shi'ite leader, Dr. Ayad Allawi, who led a political coalition friendly to Sunni Arab interests and concerns. In this environment, Riyadh was widely believed to have provided funds to Dr. Allawi for his organization's electioneering efforts.[185] Prime Minster Maliki was particularly incensed about this possibility and warned against the influence of money coming from

Saudi Arabia, the UAE, and other Arab countries.[186] Conversely, some Sunni politicians and secular leaders maintain that Iraqi Shi'ite parties accept substantial instruction, as well as money, from the Iranians.[187] Ayad Allawi has been particularly critical of Iranian meddling in Iraqi politics and complained that Iran interfered quite heavily in the political negotiations that followed that election.[188] The March 2010 election was inconclusive and underscored the fact that Iraq remains deeply divided on sectarian and ethnic lines.[189] Prime Minister Maliki noted this himself when he stated that the nation had returned to square one on the issue of sectarianism in the aftermath of the election.[190]

The *Iraqiyah* bloc under Dr. Allawi has strongly criticized Prime Minister Maliki and his allies for failing to defend Iraqi interests in interactions with Iran. These politicians specifically charge that Maliki has failed to address Iranian military incursions into Iraqi territory or the bombardment of Iraqi Kurdish villages by Iranian forces. The *Iraqiyah* bloc also maintains that Iran has diverted water from rivers flowing into Iraq so that they are virtually dry by the time they reach Iraq.[191] Sunni Iraqis have sometimes demonstrated against Iranian leaders visiting Iraq to indicate their community's distrust of Tehran.[192] More alarmingly, the *New York Times* has reported that members of the pro-U.S. Sunni Awakening Councils are reestablishing links to Sunni insurgents, including al-Qaeda, as a way of hedging their bets against an oppressive Shi'ite majority government once the United States has withdrawn its military forces from Iraq.[193] Some observers have suggested that Saudi Arabia has been providing financial support to some of Iraq's major Sunni tribes, including those involved with the Awakening movement.[194] Saudi Arabia has attempted to mediate among Iraqi factions under the umbrella of the Irbil initiative, which sought to bring Iraqi political factions together to form a coalition government.

Iraq's Shi'ite dominated government has maintained a number of disagreements with Saudi Arabia into the era of the Arab Spring. Strong Iraqi criticism of both Bahrain and Saudi Arabia over the crackdown also led to a GCC decision to request the cancelation of an Arab League Summit Conference to be hosted in Baghdad in 2011.[195] This action further angered the Iraqi leadership, many of whom viewed the Summit as an important step towards Iraq's reintegration into the Arab World as the U.S. occupation of that country draws to an end. A compromise settlement led to a decision to postpone the Summit until March 2012 because of the turmoil in the region, with the location to remain in Baghdad.[196] Large numbers of Iraqi Shi'ite citizens were also deeply angered by the Saudi intervention in Bahrain. A leading Iraqi Shi'ite newspaper called for a boycott of Saudi goods to protest the intervention in Bahrain.[197] Shi'ites throughout Iraq held demonstrations against the Saudi intervention in cities including Baghdad, Basra, and Najaf.[198]

Sectarian problems therefore remain serious within Iraq, and are of concern to both Saudi Arabia and Iran. After the United States withdraws the remainder of its military forces from Iraq, it will be difficult for Saudi Arabia and the other Sunni Gulf monarchies to remain passive should Iran continue to arm Shi'ite militias.[199] Previously, the most important power opposing Iranian influence within Iraq was the United States, but the removal of all or most U.S. military forces from that country will have some impact on U.S. ability to counter this influence. In the past, Saudi Arabia could rely on the United States to oppose Tehran without seeking to use its own influence. Moreover, any high profile Saudi activism in Iraq prior to the U.S. withdrawal threatened to irritate that United States, which has been supportive of Prime Minister Maliki, a leader whom the Saudis deeply distrust.

Conclusions.

The Saudi-Iranian rivalry is a central feature in the Middle Eastern security landscape that reaches into both the Gulf region and the Arab-Israeli theater. It is therefore a reality that will touch upon the interests of the United States in a number of situations. In many instances, Saudi opposition to Iran will serve U.S. interests, but this will not occur under all circumstances. Saudi Arabia remains a deeply anti-revolutionary state, with values and priorities that sometimes overlap with those of Washington on matters of strategic interest, and often conflict over matters of reform and democracy for other Middle Eastern states. Additionally, Middle East regional politics do not consist of rigid blocs that can be viewed as a miniature cold war, even in cases where sectarian differences are involved. With these parameters in mind, this monograph makes the following recommendations.

1. The United States must understand that the differences between Saudi Arabia and Iran will be reflected elsewhere in the Middle East, particularly in Iraq and Lebanon. In this regard, it is possible that the United States will not be the most influential external power interacting with the Iraqi government. Nevertheless, the U.S. leadership may have to decide what kind of Saudi Arabian behavior it is willing to accept in Iraq if Riyadh chooses to support Iraq's Sunni Arab population against a Shi'ite-dominated government in Baghdad. In the future, it is possible that Saudi Arabia will consider a policy of ignoring the efforts of potentially increasing numbers of its citizens to infiltrate Iraq and fight beside Iraq's Sunni Arabs if a bloody intercommunal conflict breaks out. Riyadh will be given increased freedom to do this by the U.S. military withdrawal, which would end the possibility for Saudi infiltrators to strike at U.S. targets in Iraq. Such intervention may be an inevitable response to intercommunal warfare, but cannot end well for either the United States or Saudi Arabia since a new crop of radicals will be generated to bedevil civilized nations throughout the world, possibly for decades to come. Therefore, the United States must seek to deescalate conflict among Iraqi communities before such a scenario can play out.

2. U.S. intelligence officials and policymakers must also be aware of the possibility that Saudi Arabia may overestimate Iranian involvement in any regional crisis and may conflate Shi'ite assertiveness with Iranian activism on the basis of very little evidence. Such concerns may reflect an honest Saudi appraisal based on their own assumptions or worst-case planning, but these cannot be accepted without a skeptical examination of the evidence. In many cases, Arab Shi'ite leaders will work closely with the Iranians, but not always. This problem of overestimating Iranian influence appears to be present to some extent in Saudi evaluations of both the Houthi rebellion in northern Yemen and the situation in Bahrain immediately prior to the March 2011 Saudi-led military intervention. Iran has shown an interest in the conflicts in Bahrain and Yemen, but there is a lack of conclusive evidence of Iranian involvement beyond the levels of propaganda and diplomacy. While Iran could become more involved in each of these conflicts, it appears to be a secondary player at the current time.

3. The United States needs to recognize that Saudi Arabia will seek to support conservative regimes in the Gulf, such as Bahrain, and that this Saudi support may come regardless of other governments' willingness to engage in human rights abuse, especially against Shi'ites. The United States should distance itself from such policies by continuing to call for reform. While Saudi Arabia is a friend and partner to the United States, U.S. leaders cannot remain unconcerned about repression based on sectarianism. Such repression is an open invitation to radicalization and the expansion of Iranian influence. It also inflames the situation in Iraq.

4. U.S. military training for GCC states, including Saudi Arabia, must have a strong human rights component. This should include both training provided in the GCC countries, and military education and training provided in the United States. The importance of this training must be stressed for both moral and practical reasons. It should be presented to U.S. allies as a valuable tool that will allow them to reduce the potency of Iranian propaganda and attempts at subversion. Repression against Shi'ites can honestly be portrayed as playing into Iranian hands. Also, when dealing with foreign military officers, U.S. trainers and educators should avoid accusatory approaches and indicate that respect for human rights is simply good strategic planning.

5. The U.S. civilian and military leadership must be aware of the fact that Saudi influence is not always an effective counterweight to Iranian activism in many instances, including those where U.S.-Saudi interests overlap. While Saudi Arabia usually attempts to influence its neighbors by using money and diplomacy, Iran is much more willing to fund radical militias in states that have weak central governments and a large Shi'ite community, including pro-Iranian elements. The foremost model of this policy, serving to advance Iranian interests, is Hezbollah in Lebanon, a strong and reliable Iranian ally. This policy is also apparent in the creation of the Special Groups in Iraq. In both cases, the establishment of militias has helped pro-Iranian elements not only operate as open allies of Tehran, but also to become influential players within the national government. In Lebanon, Hezbollah is the most important and influential political organization with its members and allies currently dominating the government. In Iraq the pro-Iranian groups have not achieved this level of power, but Tehran is clearly seeking to empower them towards that goal. Tehran will also be willing to put a great deal more effort and resources into an attempt to dominate Iraq since Baghdad's concerns and ambitions directly touch upon Iranian core interests in a way that activities in Lebanon almost never do. These efforts will have to be countered by the United States in conjunction with its regional partners.

6. The United States must remain aware that local powers such as Saudi Arabia are sometimes viewed as overbearing by even their closest allies. The United States may, at times, have a stake in providing a friendly counterweight to Saudi Arabia for states seeking to emphasize their independent streak. This effort will sometimes be tricky, and U.S. policy will have to be adjusted on a case-by-case basis. In general, the small Gulf States view Saudi Arabia as one of their most important allies, but believe that they will have more freedom of action on a variety of important issues if they have more than one important ally.

7. **The United States leadership must also understand that many countries concerned about Iran are nevertheless reluctant to confront such a powerful regional state.** U.S. officials sometimes complain that Saudi and other Gulf officials are unwilling to say the same things in public as they do in private about such issues as the Iranian nuclear weapons program and Iranian sponsorship of terrorism. This may be true, but Riyadh and the smaller capitals have a vested interest in not returning to the 1980s pattern of relations, which involved virulent propaganda, constant acts of subversion, and serious efforts to disrupt and cause casualties at the Hajj. The United States will therefore have to understand when a firm stand is possible for these states and when it is problematic.

8. **The U.S. military should be prepared for possible new relations with a post-Assad government in Syria so long as that government does not seek to threaten Israel.** If President Assad is overthrown, the United States may seek to work with Saudi Arabia and other friendly states to make certain that Syrian ties to Iran do not survive the transition. This effort may require the development of low level military ties including military education and training so long as Damascus appears to be interested in peace and democracy. In this regard, it might be remembered that Sadat's Egypt formed an important civilian and military relationship with the United States prior to its peace treaty with Israel. These ties helped to pave the way to that treaty, but they could not go beyond a certain point until the peace treaty became a reality.

9. **The United States military should consider the need to continue working with the Bahraini military for the time being to help prevent Bahrain from becoming a total Saudi satellite, so long as the United**

States makes progress in pushing for improvements to the Bahraini human rights situation. The U.S. ability to moderate repression and encourage reform will be diminished, or even ended, if the United States withdraws its forces, and no other nation is capable of performing even a limited role in pressuring the Bahraini government to show moderation in its governance. Training opportunities for Bahraini military personnel should, whenever possible, stress human rights issues. Military leaders within the Bahraini military with known human rights problems in their background should not be allowed to participate in U.S.-sponsored military education and training programs.

10. The United States should strongly encourage Gulf States, including Saudi Arabia, to support large-scale anti-poverty programs for Bahraini Shi'ites who currently have solid reasons for giving up on the political system and turning to Iran for help. The deplorable living conditions of many Shi'ites are a reminder of what this community believes is unrelenting discrimination against them by a Sunni minority. Strong jobs and anti-poverty programs could help improve relations between the communities and ease the process of reconciliation and national dialogue. Since Bahrain's total population is less than one million citizens, targeted economic aid could go a long way in easing suffering there.

11. The United States must use what influence it has to encourage Iraq to treat Sunni Arabs fairly, and thereby prevent intercommunal warfare that would almost certainly involve supporting roles for Iran and Saudi Arabia. The fragmented political mosaic of Iraq is a perfect context for these differences to play themselves out if Iraqi political leaders fail to act with

wisdom and tolerance. The United States will have to work closely with Saudi Arabia on Iraq policy. Saudi Arabia is, nevertheless, an imperfect partner for U.S. efforts to promote stability in Iraq, and the United States must not be distracted from efforts to mediate and resolve differences at an early stage, while recognizing the rights and claims of all parties to any Iraqi internal conflicts.

12. The United States should continue to pursue the Middle East Peace Process for both its intrinsic value and to moderate tendencies within states such as Saudi Arabia, while seeking to undermine Iran's efforts to enhance its role in Lebanon and the Palestinian territories. The Iranians prosper when they are able to portray themselves as the champions of Palestinian and Lebanese forces opposing what they maintain is an aggressive Israel. They are diminished when they are seen as seeking to disrupt a viable peace process.

13. The U.S. Army should keep the U.S. Congress particularly well informed about the value of its training mission for Lebanon, and any problems that mission faces because of the Mikati government and its Hezbollah allies, but it should not assume that military cooperation with Lebanon is no longer possible. Lebanon has special problems with sectarianism that make its military different from a Western military. Lebanese government requirements for the military to take significant action in the interests of only one sect or political trend could lead to the collapse of the military as an institution. It will only become an effective instrument for repression if it is thoroughly purged, which probably cannot happen without inciting civil unrest. The severing of U.S. ties to the Lebanese military could demoralize Western-oriented officers within that organization while raising the importance of the Hezbollah militia forces to the Lebanese defense. These forces will continue to be well-armed and equipped by Iran.

14. The U.S. diplomats and military leaders dealing with Iraq must be prepared for Iranian attempts to take advantage of serious disagreements between Saudi Arabia and Iraq after Washington withdraws its troops from that country. To contain Iran while supporting stability and democracy, the United States must be prepared to mediate between Saudi Arabia and Iraq, and limit Iranian efforts to insert itself into such a process. Since key Saudi concerns may involve Iraqi government actions in Sunni Arab areas, the United States will have to be aware of issues in those areas, and it will have to be prepared to support measures to increase Sunni Arab willingness to participate in the political system along with a Shi'ite and Kurdish willingness to share power.

15. The United States should remain aware of political changes that might occur in Iran in the hope that meaningful dialogue on security issues may become possible at some point. The failure of the Green Revolution in 2009 was a serious disappointment to many Americans and other supporters of liberal, democratic government. Nevertheless, the last chapter may not have been written in this story. The examples of Egypt, Tunisia, and Libya are already of considerable concern to Tehran. In these times of revolutionary upheaval, the United States must continue to point out the hypocrisy and opportunism of the Iranian regime on issues such as Syrian repression.

ENDNOTES

1. Officials of some Gulf Arab states have used this description in an exasperated way in discussions with the author. Also see King Abdullah, "Eldest brother of Egypt: Sharaf," *Saudi Gazette*, April 24, 2011.

2. At the time of this writing, it appears that Jordan and Morocco have an excellent chance of being admitted into the GCC. Neither of these two countries has the geographical or financial profile of the current members, but it is likely that the current GCC states hoped to help shore up these states and their monarchial governments during the "Arab Spring." See "GCC Welcomes Jordan, Morocco membership," *Kuwait Times*, May 11, 2011.

3. On recent Saudi efforts to influence King Abdullah of Jordan against reform, see Paul Richter and Neela Banerjee, "U.S.-Saudi Rivalry Intensifies," *Los Angeles Times*, June 19, 2011.

4. The term "Wahhabi" is almost never used in the Arabian Peninsula, although the other more preferred terms are confusing and do not clearly delineate these individuals from other religious conservatives. See Christopher M. Blanchard, *The Islamic Traditions of Wahhabism and Salafiyya*, Washington, DC: Congressional Research Service, 2008, p. 2.

5. Thomas Hegghammer, *Jihad in Saudi Arabia: Violence and Pan-Islamism since 1979*, Cambridge, UK: Cambridge University Press, 2010, pp. 17-18.

6. Toby Jones, "The Iraq Effect in Saudi Arabia," *Middle East Report*, Winter 2005, pp. 20-25; "Mutawwa accused of beating Shiites," *Kuwait Times*, August 6, 2007.

7. "US wants to divide and rule Muslims: Iran," *Arab News*, December 5, 2010.

8. "S. Arabia 'does not advocate military action against Iran'," *Jordan Times*, February 17, 2010.

9. Michael Buchanan, "Saudi Arabia: Calls for political reform muted," BBC News, May 24, 2011. On Iran's stolen election, see Hooman Majid, *The Ayatollah's Democracy: An Iranian Challenge*, New York: W.W. Norton & Co., 2010, especially pp. 48-66.

10. Graham E. Fuller, *The 'Center of the Universe' The Geopolitics of Iran*, Boulder, CO: Westview Press, 1991, Chap. 6.

11. Henner Furtig, *Iran's Rivalry with Saudi Arabia Between the Gulf Wars*, Reading, UK: Ithaca Press, 2006, p. 37.

12. Kenneth M. Pollack, *The Persian Puzzle: The Conflict Between Iran and America*, New York: Random House, 2004, p. 199.

13. Scott Peterson, *Let the Swords Encircle Me: Iran – A Journey Behind the Headlines*, New York: Simon & Schuster, 2010, p. 106.

14. Fuller, p. 106.

15. Ray Tekeyh, *Guardians of the Revolution: Iran and the World in the Age of the Ayatollahs*, Oxford, UK: Oxford University Press, 2009, pp. 198-199.

16. "S. Arabia 'does not advocate military action against Iran'."

17. See, for example, Mark Landler, "Clinton Raises U.S. Concerns of Military Power in Iran," *Washington Post*, February 16, 2010.

18. Yochi J. Dreazen and Margaret Coker, "Gates Seeks Help from Gulf Leaders on Iran Sanctions," *Wall Street Journal*, March 12, 2010, p. 15.

19. Willem van Kemenade, "Which way will China lean on Iran?" *Daily Star*, (Beirut), October 8, 2010.

20. Jay Solomon, "Saudi Suggests 'Squeezing' Iran over Nuclear Ambitions," *Wall Street Journal*, June 22, 2011; "Saudi will seek nuclear arms if Iran gets them," *Gulf Times*, July 1, 2011.

21. "Iran says it uncovers second cyber attack," *Daily Star,* April 25, 2011.

22. Michael Birnbaum, "Egypt Shows Signs of New Assertiveness Abroad," *Washington Post*, April 28, 2011.

23. Ernesto Londono and Joel Greenberg, "Egypt's Rulers to Reopen Gaza Crossing in Days," *Washington Post*, May 26, 2011.

24. "Govt tries to calm sectarian tensions," *Kuwait Times*, September 15, 2010.

25. "MPs File to Question Kuwait PM over Pro-Iranian Remarks," *The Peninsula*, May 23, 2011; B. Izzak, "MPs file motion to oust PM over Iran," *Kuwait Times*, June 15, 2011.

26. *Ibid.*

27. "King Abdullah slams acts of 'Fitnah' in Egypt," *Saudi Gazette*, January 30, 2011.

28. *Ibid.*

29. "Saudi Arabia Urges peaceful resolution of Egypt Crisis," *Arab News*, February 8, 2011.

30. Scott Peterson, "Iran's Khamenei praises Egyptian protesters declares 'Islamic Awakening,'" *Christian Science Monitor*, February 4, 2011.

31. Ali Akbar Dareini, "Iran leader: West cannot 'confiscate' Arab Spring," *Daily Star* (Beirut), August 31, 2011.

32. "Iran seeks brave move from Egypt to resume ties," *Jordan Times*, April 24, 2011.

33. "Egypt: Iran ties will not undermine Gulf Security," *Kuwait Times*, April 27, 2011.

34. "Regional Turmoil in Focus at Saudi King's Talks with Egypt," *Arab News*, April 26, 2011.

35. "$4 Billion Saudi Aid for Egypt," *Arab News*, May 22, 2011.

36. "Qatar plans $10 billion in Egypt projects," *Saudi Gazette*, May 25, 2011.

37. "GCC Ministers to discuss Jordan's membership bid." *Kuwait Times*, August 28, 2011.

38. See "Yemen Leader's Role Presents Thorny Issues for US," *New York Times*, January 5, 2010; Jane's Sentinel Country Risk Assessments, "Yemen: External Affairs," Jane's Information Group, January 8, 2010.

39. Oman probably has the best relations with Iran of any GCC state.

40. *Bahrain's Sectarian Challenge*, Brussels, Belgium: International Crisis Group (ICG), May 2005, p. 2.

41. *Ibid.*, pp. 2-5.

42. Yitzhak Nakash, *Reaching for Power, The Shi'a in the Modern Arab World*, Princeton and Oxford, UK: Princeton University Press, 2006, p. 34.

43. *Ibid.*, p. 50.

44. See Jones, pp. 29-32; "Saudi Shiite held after meeting King," *Kuwait Times*, May 19, 2008.

45. Lori Plotkin Boghardt, *Kuwait Amid War, Peace and Revolution 1979-1991*, New York: Palgrave MacMillan, 2006, pp. 110-119.

46. *Ibid.*, Chap. 6.

47. "Kuwaitis, Iranians among sleeper cells' members," *Kuwait Times*, August 24, 2010.

48. "Kuwait court tries alleged Iran spy cell," *Khaleej Times*, October 13, 2010.

49. This sentence can still be appealed to the Kuwaiti Supreme Court. See "Death for Three Iran Spies in Kuwait," *Gulf Times*, March 30, 2011.

50. "Three get death in Iran Spy Ring," *Kuwait Times*, March 30, 2011.

51. Fouad al-Obaid, "Regional Powder Keg," *Kuwait Times*, April 4, 2011.

52. Reuters, "Bahrain tries 2 Iranians, Bahraini in Iran spy case," Gulf Research Center, *Gulf in the Media Electronic Newsletter*, April 13, 2011.

53. "Ahmadinejad denies spy rings in Kuwait," *Kuwait Times*, April 5, 2011.

54. "Yemen's War: Pity those caught in the Middle," *Economist*, November 21, 2009, p. 49.

55. *Yemen: Defusing the Saada Time Bomb*, Brussels, Belgium: ICG, May 27, 2009, p. 12.

56. *Ibid.*, p. 10.

57 ."Saudis held briefly by Yemeni rebels," *Arab News*, April 25, 2010.

58. Mohamed Ghobari and Raissa Kasolowsky, "Yemen's al Qaeda calls for jihad, fighting in north," Reuters, February 8, 2010.

59. "Saudi Air Force hits Yemen rebels after border raid," *Jordan Times*, November 6, 2009.

60. Robert F. Worth, "Yemen Seems to Reject Cease-Fire with Rebels," *New York Times*, February 1, 2010.

61. "No Changes in border with Yemen, says Prince Khaled," *Arab News*, March 7, 2010.

62. Tore T. Petersen, *Richard Nixon, Great Britain and the Anglo-American Alignment in the Persian Gulf and Arabian Peninsula:*

Making Allies out of Clients, Brighton, UK: Sussex Academic Press, 2009, p. 50.

63. See Fred H. Lawson, *Bahrain: The Modernization of Autocracy*, Boulder, CO: Westview Press, 1989, p. 123; and Anthony H. Cordesman, *Bahrain, Oman, Qatar, and the UAE: Challenges of Security*, Boulder, CO: Westview Press, 1997, p. 41.

64. Lawson, pp. 128-129.

65 ."Timeline: Bahrain," *BBC News: World Edition*, August 25, 2005.

66. R. K. Ramazani, "Iran's Islamic Revolution and the Persian Gulf," *Current History*, January 1985, p. 7.

67. Henner Furtig, *Iran's Rivalry with Saudi Arabia between the Gulf Wars*, Reading, UK: Ithaca Press, 2006, p. 64.

68. *Bahrain's Sectarian Challenge*, pp. 2-6.

69. M K Bhadrakumar, "Saudis Bring Iran, US closer together," *Asia Times Online*, March 18, 2011.

70. *Ibid.*

71. "Bahrain protesters seek to oust the royal family," *Kuwait Times*, February 22, 2011.

72. Neela Banerjee "As Cries for Revolution fade, Bahrainis wonder what went wrong," *Los Angeles Times*, April 15, 2011.

73. "Gulf Business hub Bahrain faces uncertain future," *Kuwait Times*, March 24, 2011.

74. "Bahrain king offers reform talks in July," *Kuwait Times*, June 1, 2011.

75. "Tension rises as GCC asks UN to curb Iran," *Gulf Times*, April 19, 2011.

76. "Bahrain puts down foreign plot," United Press International, March 21, 2011.

77. Bahrain tells 16 Lebanese to leave, 5 gone: diplomat," *Daily Star*, April 4, 2011.

78. *Ibid.*

79. Alex Delmar-Morgan, "Bahrain to Ease Restraints," *Wall Street Journal*, May 9, 2011.

80. "Bahrain to reassert its control over mosques," *Gulf Times*, September 7, 2010; and "Shi'ite mosque demolitions raise tension in Bahrain, *Kuwait Times*, April 23, 2011.

81. "Bahraini Opposition flays government crackdown," *Arab News*, April 24, 2011.

82. Joby Warrick and Michael Birnbaum, "Questions as Bahrain Stifles Revolt," *Washington Post*, April 15, 2011.

83. Paul Richter, "Bahrain Backs Away from Ban on Two Shiite Political Groups," *Los Angeles Times*, April 16, 2011; "Bahrain not trying to disband opposition groups" *Khaleej Times*, April 16, 2011.

84. "Respect our Unity, GCC tells Tehran," *Kuwait Times*, April 21, 2011.

85. "Gulf Arabs Discuss Iran 'Meddling'," *The Nation* (Pakistan) April 4, 2011.

86. "GCC to turn new leaf in relations with Tehran," *Kuwait Times*, April 23, 2011.

87. Reuters, "Bahrain tries 2 Iranians, Bahraini in Iran spy case."

88. On the development of this relationship, see Patrick Seele, *Asad: The Struggle for the Middle East*, Berkeley and Los Angeles, CA: University of California Press, 1988, Chap. 21. Also see Hugh Naylor, "Syria, Seeking Investors, Turns Cautiously to Iran," *New York Times*, October 4, 2007.

89. Seele, pp. 351-354.

90. Matthew Tempest, "'No Plans' to invade Syria, Insists Blair," *Guardian*, April 14 2003; David Ignatius, "Iran and Syria are just waiting the Bush administration out," *Daily Star*, July 25, 2008.

91. "New U.S. warning to Syria on Scuds," BBC News, May 5, 2010.

92. Agence France-Presse, "Iran warns Israel against attacking Syria," Gulf Research Center, May 1, 2010.

93. The author has spoken to a number of Israeli military officials on this issue.

94. Christopher Torchia, "Turkey urges Syria to stop crackdown," Associated Press, April 28, 2011.

95. Reuters, "Signs of Thaw Between Syria and Iraq PM Maliki," Gulf Research Center, Gulf in the News, September 15, 2010.

96. "Iraq's Shiites grudgingly back Syria's Baath," *Kuwait Times*, April 26, 2011.

97. *Reshuffling the Cards? (1) Syria's Evolving Strategy,* Brussels, Belgium: ICG, 2009, p. ii.

98. "US Reacts to Fear of Iran's Rising Clout," *Wall Street Journal*, March 22, 2011.

99. See Lawrence Freedman and Efraim Karsh, *The Gulf Conflict 1990-91*, Princeton, NJ: Princeton University Press, 1993, p. 96.

100. Office of the White House Press Secretary, "Joint Statement by President Bush and Saudi Crown Prince Abdullah," Washington, DC: The White House, April 25, 2005, available from *georgewbush-whitehouse.archives.gov*.

101. Mirella Hodeib and Hassan Lakiss, "'Window of Hope' opens in Lebanon crisis," *Daily Star*, January 20, 2011.

102. *Ibid.*

103. "Syria, Iran underline support for Lebanon against Israel," *Jordan Times*. August 12, 2010.

104. "Ahmadinejad calls upon Syria to engage in dialogue, Kuwait News Agency, August 25, 2011; "Tehran accuses West of meddling in Syria," *Kuwait Times*, June 15, 2011.

105. "U.S. suspects Iran Bracing Syria," *Daily Star*, April 15, 2011; Nada Bakri, "Europe Accuses Iranian Force of Aiding Syrian Crackdown," *New York Times*, August 25, 2011.

106. Adam Entous and Matthew Rosenberg, "US Says Iran Helps Crackdown in Syria," *Wall Street Journal*, April 14, 2011.

107. "Iran Warns against Western Intervention in Syria," *Daily Star*, August 16, 2011.

108. "Kuwait, Bahrain follow Saudi Lead as Syrian Crackdown continues," *Arab News* (Riyadh), August 8, 2011; Nada Bakri, "3 Arab Countries Recall Ambassadors to Syria," *New York Times*, August 8, 2011.

109. *Ibid.*

110. For one aspect of this concern, see "Saudi Arabia arrests 164 anti-Syrian protesters," *Daily Star*, August 25, 2011.

111. See Marwan Muasher, *The Arab Center: The Promise of Moderation*, New Haven and London, UK: Yale University Press, 2008, Appendix 2.

112. "Tel Aviv 'Mulling Saudi Peace Plan'," *Jordan Times*, October 20, 2008.

113. The United States has spent about $600 million a year supporting the Palestinians since 2007, although the future of this support is uncertain. See Jennifer Steinhauer and Steven Lee Myers," House G.O.P. tightens its bond with Netanyahu," *New York Times*, September 20, 2011.

114. Christopher M. Blanchard, *Saudi Arabia: Background and U.S. Relations, CRS Report for Congress*, Washington, DC: Congressional Research Service, 2010. p. 32

115. Christopher M. Blanchard and Alfred B. Prados, *Saudi Arabia: Terrorist Financing Issues, CRS Report for Congress*, Washington, DC: Congressional Research Service, September 2007, p. 16.

116. *Ibid.* p. 17.

117. "Tehran 'blocking' Fatah-Hamas Reconciliation," *Kuwait Times*, March 14, 2010.

118. Barbara Slavin, *Bitter Friends, Bosom Enemies Iran, the U.S. and the Twisted Path to Confrontation*, New York: St. Martin's Press, 2007, p. 91.

119. Ronen Bergman, *The Secret War with Iran*, New York: Free Press, 2008, 270-71.

120. "IAF hits Gaza Tunnels in wake of bombing attempt by sea," *Ha'aretz*, February 2, 2010; "How Israel Foiled an Arms Convoy Bound for Hamas," *TIME*, March 30, 2009; and Barbara Opall-Rome, "Underground Weapon: Israeli Tunnel Blaster Targets Threats from Gaza Strip," *Defense News*, June 6, 2011, p. 24.

121. Joshua Mitnick, "Israel's Seizure of arms shipment highlights rising unease about Iran," *Christian Science Monitor*, March 15, 2011.

122. "The Gaza-Egypt Smuggling Tunnels must be Closed," *Wall Street Journal*, January 14, 2009.

123. Ian Black, "Gaza Blockade: Iran Offers Escort to Next Aid Convoy," *Guardian*, June 7, 2010.

124. "Iran Revolutionary Guards ready to escort Gaza ships," *Kuwait Times*, June 7, 2010.

125. "Hezbollah chief meets Ahmadinejad," BBC News, February 26, 2010.

126. "Hezbollah brought stability to Lebanon: Iranian official," *Daily Star*, June 27, 2011.

127. Bergman, Chap. 15; Augustus Richard Norton, *Hezbollah: A Short History*, Princeton and Oxford, UK: Princeton University Press, 2007, pp. 34-35.

128. Thanassis Cambanis, "Stronger Hezbollah Emboldened for Fights Ahead," *New York Times*, October 6, 2010; and Amos Harel and Amos Issacharoff, *34 Days: Israel, Hezbollah and the War in Lebanon*, New York: Palgrave, 2008, p. 48.

129. Michael R. Gordon and Andrew W. Lehran, "U.S. Strains to Stop Arms Flow," *New York Times*, December 6, 2010.

130. *Drums of War: Israel and the "Axis of Resistance,"* Brussels, Belgium: International Crisis Group, 2010, p. 6.

131. *Ibid.*

132. Michael Young, *The Ghosts of Martyrs Square: An Eyewitness Account of Lebanon's Life Struggle*, New York: Simon & Schuster, 2010, p. 67.

133. *Ibid.*, p. 67.

134. Harel and Issacharoff, pp. 241-253.

135. Morten Valbjorn and Andre Bank, "Signs of a New Arab Cold War: The 2006 Lebanon War and the Sunni-Shi'i Divide," *Middle East Report*, Spring 2007, p. 7.

136. Harel and Issacharoff, p. 249.

137. Thanassis Cambanis, "Stronger Hezbollah Emboldened for Fights Ahead," *New York Times*, October 6, 2010.

138. Babak Degghanpisheh, "Lebanon Stages a Diversion," *Newsweek*, October 25, 2010.

139. Hussein Dakroub, "Hariri slams Iranian interference," *Daily Star*, April 8, 2011.

140. *Ibid.*

141. "Siniora: Hezbollah has disregarded Saudi help," *Daily Star*, April 14, 2011.

142. "Future criticizes Nasrallah over 2006 Saudi Aid," *Daily Star*, April 13, 2011.

143. Borzou Daragahi, "Lebanon's Prime Minister Visits Iran," *Los Angeles Times*, November 28, 2010.

144. Liz Sly, "U.N. Court Indicts Hezbollah members in 2005 assassination in Lebanon, *Washington Post*, August 17, 2011.

145. Mikati is a Sunni Muslim, although he is very sensitive to Hezbollah interests. Because of Lebanon's confessional system, all prime ministers must be Sunni Muslims just as all speakers of the parliament must be Shi'ite Muslims, and all presidents must be Maronite Christians.

146. "Hezbollah rise in Lebanon gives Syria, Iran sway," *Khaleej Times*, June 14, 2011.

147. Nicholas Blanford, "An Interview with Lebanon's Prime Minister Najib Mikati," *TIME*, March 13, 2011.

148. David Ignatius, "Hezbollah's Play of Shadows," *Washington Post*, February 28, 2011.

149. "Political rivals increasingly divided on Syria," *The Daily Star*, August 10, 2011.

150. Hussein Dakroub, "Hariri praises Saudi Stance on Syrian Unrest," *The Daily Star*, August 9, 2011.

151. *Ibid.*

152. Casey L. Addis, *U.S. Security Assistance to Lebanon*, Washington, DC: Congressional Research Service, 2011, p. 3.

153. Matthew Lee "US Considers Slashing Financial Aid to Lebanon," *Washington Times*, January 26, 2011.

154. "Iran is ready to start defense funding for Lebanon: Minister," *Daily Star*, February 7, 2011.

155. Patrice Hill, "War-Weary Iraq sees economic rebound," *Washington Times*, April 11, 2011.

156. Jim Muir, "Iran's Mixed Feelings on Looming War," BBC News: World Edition, January 17, 2003.

157. These gains were short-lived as Saddam gave up all of the fruits of victory in the Iran-Iraq War after the invasion of Kuwait in order to establish diplomatic relations with Tehran and pacify his eastern front in preparation for war with the United States and its allies. See Freedman and Karsh, pp. 108-109.

158. Andrew Tilghman, "Experts: Iraq Air Force Unready," *Defense News*, January 24, 2011.

159. Anthony H. Cordesman and Martin Kleiber, *Iran's Military Forces and Warfighting Capabilities: The Threat to the Northern Gulf*, Westport, CT: Praeger, 2007, pp. 196-199.

160. Bruce Riedel, "The Mideast after Iran Gets the Bomb," *Current History*, December 2010, p. 372.

161. "Iran Denies Getting Missile Technology From N Korea," Associated Press, May 17, 2011; "Iran: Parliament Speaker to visit North Korea Sunday, underlining close ties," *Washington Post*, August 31, 2011.

162. "Iraq to purchase 36 F-16 fighter jets from U.S.," Reuters, July 30, 2011; Jim Loney, "U.S. and Iraq Talking but No F-16 Deal Yet," Reuters, August 31, 2011; Tim Craig, "Big Guns Fire Up Iraqi Army's Confidence," *Washington Post*, June 6, 2011.

163. "Iraq Keen on Rebuilding Own Army—Iraqi VP," Kuwait News Agency, August 15, 2011.

164. Bruce Riedel, "The Mideast after Iran Gets the Bomb," *Current History*, December 2010, pp. 370-375.

165. This rise of U.S. influence and involvement in both Iraq and Afghanistan occurred shortly after President George W. Bush had identified Iran as part of "an axis of evil." Such rhetoric contributed to the Iranian view that they were now being encircled by enemies led by a particularly hostile power.

166. "Iraqi President calls for strategic ties with Iran," Kuwait News Agency, March 28, 2011.

167. Thomas Erdbrink and Leila Fadel, "Maliki, Iran's Leaders Talk About the Future of Iraq's Government, *Washington Post*, October 19, 2010.

168. "Iraq's Looming new government," *Economist*, November 13, 2010, p. 57.

169. "Shiite Cleric Warns U.S. Forces to Leave," *Washington Post*, August 10, 2011.

170. On the al-Quds Force, see Cordesman and Kleiber, pp. 78-81; and "Iran's 'invisible man'," *The Middle East*, August/September 2008, pp. 28-31.

171. "Iraqi cleric threatens to revive Mehdi Army," *Kuwait Times*, April 10, 2010.

172. See Michael Knights, "The Evolution of Iran's Special Groups in Iraq," *West Point Counter Terrorism Center Sentinel*, November 2010, p. 13.

173. Aseel Kami, "US trainers could be targets: Iraq's Sadr," Reuters, August 7, 2011.

174. Ed O' Keefe," Iraq to Seek Talks to Keep American Trainers Past 2011," *Washington Post*, August 3, 2011.

175. "Moktada Al-Sadr Warns U.S. Troops to Leave Iraq," *New York Times*, August 8, 2011.

176. Michael S. Schmidt and Jack Healy, "Shiite Militia Claims Responsibility for Attack in Baghdad," *New York Times*, June 11, 2011.

177. David S. Cloud, "Panetta: Iranian weapons used to attack Americans in Iraq," *Los Angeles Times*, July 11, 2011.

178. "Iraq and Iran: Big Brother Comes to Town," *Economist*, March 8, 2008.

179. "Turkey, Iran battle for clout, deals in Iraq," *Kuwait Times*, December 9, 2010.

180. Robert Gibbons, "Saudi Says U.S. Policy is Handing Iraq to Iran," Reuters, September 21, 2005.

181. "No More Gestures to Saudis: Maliki," Agence France-Presse, May 29, 2009.

182. Tarek al-Issawi, "Report: Iran appoints ambassador to Iraq," *Associated Press*, May 10, 2006.

183. "Maliki Rules Out more gestures to Saudi Arabia," *Daily Star*, May 29, 2009.

184. Viola Gienger, "Gates Urges Gulf States to 'Embrace' Iraq to put Brakes on Iran," *Bloomberg.com*, June 23, 2009.

185. "Ahmadinejad, Saudi King hold more phone talks: IRNA," Associated Free Press, October 21, 2010.

186. Anthony Shadid, "Maliki Creates Coalition to Compete in Iraqi Vote," *Washington Post*, October 2, 2009.

187. Daniel W. Smith, "Iraqis Stay Silent on Protests in Iran," *Washington Times*, July 9, 2009.

188. "Allawi accuses Iran over election," BBC News, March 30, 2010; Ayad Allawi, "How Iraq can Fortify its Fragile Democracy," *Washingtonpost.com*, June 10, 2010.

189. Michael S. Schmidt and Tim Arango, "Bitter Feud Between Top Iraqi Leaders Stalls Government, *New York Times*, June 26, 2011.

190. Steven Lee Myers, "As Maliki Clings to Power, Iraq's Fissures Deepen," *New York Times*, October 3, 2010.

191. "Iraqi List threatens to withdraw confidence from Maliki's government," Kuwait News Agency, July 21, 2011.

192. "Iraqis protest visit of ex-Iranian president," *Kuwait Times*, March 5, 2009; and "Iraq and Iran," *Economist*, March 8, 2008, p. 55.

193. Timothy Williams and Duraid Adnan, "Sunnis in Iraq Allied with U.S. Quitting to Rejoin Rebels," *New York Times*, October 17, 2010.

194. Christopher M. Blanchard, *Saudi Arabia: Background and U.S. Relations*, Washington, DC: Congressional Research Service, June 2010.

195. "Fate of Baghdad Summit to be decided by Arab League FMs," *Jordan Times*, April 15, 2011.

196. "Arab League delays summit by year to March 2012," *Khaleej Times*, May 6, 2011.

197. "Iraqis call for Boycott of Saudi goods over Bahrain," *Kuwait Times*, March 21, 2011; "Iraq's own sectarian divide remembered," *Kuwait Times*, April 24, 2011.

198. "Iraqis protest GCC Troops in Bahrain," Reuters, March 20, 2011.

199. Helene Cooper, "Saudis Say they might back Sunnis if U.S. leaves Iraq," *New York Times*, December 13, 2006.

U.S. ARMY WAR COLLEGE

Major General Gregg F. Martin
Commandant

*****

STRATEGIC STUDIES INSTITUTE

Director
Professor Douglas C. Lovelace, Jr.

Director of Research
Dr. Antulio J. Echevarria II

Author
Dr. W. Andrew Terrill

Director of Publications
Dr. James G. Pierce

Publications Assistant
Ms. Rita A. Rummel

*****

Composition
Mrs. Jennifer E. Nevil

www.ingramcontent.com/pod-product-compliance
Lightning Source LLC
Chambersburg PA
CBHW060152290526
45789CB00003B/1015